Your
Dream
Relationship

Your Dream Relationship

Eleven Steps to Finding Unconditional Love

ALIX ∞ RONALD GAVRAN

Blue Dolphin Publishing
1993

Published by Blue Dolphin Publishing, Inc.
P.O. Box 1920, Nevada City, CA 95959

ISBN: 0-931892-75-9

Library of Congress Cataloging-in-Publication Data

Gavran, Alix, 1951-
    Your dream relationship : eleven steps to finding
unconditional love / Alix ∞ Ronald Gavran.
        p. cm.
    ISBN 0-931892-75-9 : $10.00
    1. Man-woman relationships. 2. Interpersonal relations.
3. Mate selection. 4. Self-help techniques.
I. Gavran, Ronald, 1943-   II. Title.
HQ801.G38 1993
306.7—dc20   93-27333
                                                            CIP

Printed in the United States of America by
Blue Dolphin Press, Inc., Grass Valley, California
10   9   8   7   6   5   4   3   2   1

If you wish to receive a copy of the latest
Blue Dolphin Publishing catalogue of books
and to be placed on our mailing list,
please send us this card.

PLEASE PRINT

Book in which this card was found _____

NAME _____

ADDRESS _____

CITY _____ STATE _____

ZIP / POSTAL CODE _____ COUNTRY _____

BLUE DOLPHIN PUBLISHING, INC.

Mailing List
P.O. Box 1908
Nevada City, CA 95959-1908

We dedicate this book to all men & women
on our planet Earth.

May your hearts be opened
to the truth within you.

May Your Dream Relationship
be realized
in unconditional love.

Table of Contents

Acknowledgments

Our recognition of, respect, and devotion to
The Divine that permeates all.

Our profound gratitude to our parents:
Evelyn & John S. Gavran and
Jeanny & Jean-Pierre Mores (in spirit since Dec., 1985)
for their love and understanding, and for pointing us toward
a path of righteousness.

Our heart-filled thanks to Chris Griscom for her wonderful
work that brought us to New Mexico, and for facilitating the
joining of our spirits at our marriage ceremony.

Our deepest appreciation to Lea Sanders for her guiding wisdom, inspiring encouragement and loving friendship.

Our most sincere gratitude to Cora Belle Ogilvie for exempli-
fying to us unconditional love, spiritual sharing, and unselfish
service.

Our loving thanks to each and every person we've come into
contact with in this lifetime, and for having shared in our life
lessons.

Our sincere appreciation and gratitude to Paul Clemens for his
expertise and encouraging support and to Corinn Codye for
her valuable editing.

Word to the Reader

Both of us had gone through disappointing relationships. Some had been short and/or painful, others filled with struggle and misunderstanding, all of which had finally broken up. After these failed relationships, we also, unknown to each other, had gone through the eleven steps that we share with you in this book.

These eleven steps prepared us on a very deep inner level to join in a relationship of unconditional love. Our coming together seemed effortless because we were ready for this event. The eleven-step process itself was initiated by an inner prompting to be true to our innerselves and to change everything in our lives gradually for the better. We had fallen in love with the process—how wonderful we felt within our discoveries and transformations—and were not focused on results. We did not know where we were headed, nor when we would get there. Now we know that the process was refining and tuning us for our dream relationship.

The outcome of our eleven-step process has been far greater than we could ever have imagined. We have come home to our innerselves, our essence, that resourceful, dimensionless flow of energy uniquely formed in each of us. It originates from a source of unconditional love, peace, righteousness, truth, acceptance and knowledge which has been imparted to each of us. The innerself is all that we truly are. We've experienced a sense of deep trust in our innerselves that adds immense happiness and inner peace. Our dream relationship brought forth and clearly defined our life's work/purpose—serving and helping others to help themselves.

When we came together, we experienced a knowing between us that we would create "something new." After we were newly married, one of our teachers said, "You have a relationship that needs to be shared with the world." He saw our dream relationship, our unconditional love, and acknowledged it.

The time has come, within our universal flow, to share this "something new" that we have created, and how we prepared ourselves to make our dream relationship a daily reality. We sincerely believe you can too! It is *your choice* and will take *your commitment.*

We want to emphasize that you will create *YOUR* dream relationship, not a copy of ours. Each of us creates our own reality. The eleven-step process is a tool for your creation. It worked perfectly for us—it can work for you! Keep in mind that it applies to all types of relationships.

Each of us is a divine being, a powerful creator that orchestrates our going through the eleven-step process in our own way and at our own pace. This inner journey is exclusive to each and every one, along with many individual discoveries and transformations.

From the depths of our hearts we wish you all the rewards on your journey to discover your innerself and create *YOUR* dream relationship.

With Love & Peace,
Alix ∞ Ronald Gavran

A "dream" relationship is no longer
a playground for image-games, is no longer
a battlefield, nor a treadmill—it is bliss.

Introduction

Before we introduce the dream relationship, let's look at relationship. A relationship is a conscious decision and commitment by two people to join together in meeting life's experiences. At times we enter relationships under the pretense of love, while masking insecurity and/or a fear of being alone, and/or a feeling of not being whole. We look for the other person to provide what we lack and often don't see ourselves as whole. It is important to know that each of us is whole within ourselves. On a much deeper level, a relationship is also an unconscious attempt to realize a step towards a memory that we carry from eons of time—oneness. It is a most natural attempt to live this memory with another human being.

In many relationships, however, images and personality traits clash, expectations don't get fulfilled, feelings get hurt, co-dependency becomes established, love is conditioned, concessions are made, jealousy, possessiveness and control surface and on and on. The unconscious attempt to realize a step towards oneness ends up in a playground for image-games, a ground where old patterns are replayed over and over again, where karmic debts are repaid and created—a never-ending treadmill. And that is okay—it is neither bad nor good—it is a way to learn our lessons on our journey. Learning our lessons doesn't necessarily mean staying on the treadmill forever, but learning and moving on.

So, let's step off that treadmill and get ready for a quantum leap, because we want to go a step further—to a dream relationship. A "dream" relationship is a *conscious step* towards oneness, unlike a relationship, which is the *unconscious attempt* to realize a step towards oneness. *It is a joining of two beings in a free-flowing dance, accepting one another, and giving each other permission to be who they inwardly are, consciously creating a "third entity" called the "relationship," where their essences merge and become one and where unconditional love resides.* The "dream" relationship exists on an essence level and is far beyond and above the "physical" personalities of the two beings involved.

We've learned that it is very important to create the relationship as a "third entity," which is neither us, nor our partner, but is not separate. It is the fusion of our essences—one. We can also look at it from the point of view of creation: whenever two are joined, a third is created!

From our own experience, we can assure you that this type of relationship is no longer a playground for image-games, is no longer a battlefield, nor a treadmill—it is bliss! Let us show you why.

In a "treadmill" relationship, we stand as opposites on a playground or battlefield and try to resolve or fight over our personality problems. We blame each other for what we do to each other, not realizing that we are only a mirror for one another. In other words, when someone challenges us physically, mentally or emotionally, our reactions reveal what is inside us. When there is anger inside, we express anger. When there is love inside, we express love. The other person does not make us angry. Instead, the other person mirrors (makes us aware of) our anger. Being involved in constantly mirroring each other, we never get to the real place of relationship, because we never created it. It becomes a purely physical game, absent of who we really are.

On the other hand, a dream relationship is like a triangle, where we and our partner stand at both ends of the base of the triangle and the relationship is the pinnacle of the triangle, way above. When personality issues come up in a dream relationship, we know that it is our "stuff" and has nothing to do with our partner and will never affect the relationship, which is far above all that "stuff." The relationship is that place of unconditional love where we and our partner go to experience peace, bliss, ecstasy and the knowing that it is timeless and dimensionless. We must understand that the relationship, the place we go to, is not a place outside of us. It is our innermost core.

Are you ready for the journey to *YOUR* dream relationship? We believe that it is in everybody's potential to create exactly that—*YOUR* dream relationship. In the following chapters we give you tools to use in a way that fits you best in creating your just rewards.

The eleven steps to *YOUR* dream relationship are a process of innerself discovery. Accessing the innerself, that resourceful, dimensionless flow of energy originating from a source of unconditional love, peace, righteousness, truth, acceptance and knowledge, provides an important thrust to our quest for true relationship. The physical body enables the expression of the innerself and its inherent source. The human behavior of denial is often accompanied by ignorance and jealousy in the form of greed, hatred, anger and destruction. None of these behavioral expressions are within our definition of the innerself. These denial-induced behaviors often run rampant without our slightest concern for the important innerself. Discovering the innerself and implementing its messages promise to bring continuity and essential direction to our lives. The eleven-step process is about changing the outer-directed perception of ourselves to become the very innerself. It is about manifesting this innerself in the outer world to achieve an agreeable flow. It is about listening to the innerself dwelling in the heart and quieting the busy, active mind long enough to let the innerself take charge.

The eleven-step process is the journey itself—from outward to inward. Therefore it is advisable to start with the outward physical steps sequenced from one to four. These four outward steps provide the sense of well-being, the greater awareness of physical necessities and liabilities, the strength, the clarity, the happiness and the higher energy level needed to support us in the inwardly-directed steps five to eleven. Since these inward steps are interrelated, you may experience working on any one of them, some of them or all of them, at any given time. Our experience revealed that it was essential to practice all eleven steps.

Please understand that no step is higher or lower than another, that Step Eleven is not more "evolved" than Step Four, or Step Five less "evolved" than Step Nine. They are one-in-all and all-in-one. There is no separation. We had to put them in some sort of sequence to be able to give you an outline to work with.

We have also included some of our experiences as examples to help you see how the steps worked for us.

This process asks for a full commitment and is not the basic light-switch technique, off and on in seconds. It is a major process that will take time. It taught us to be process-oriented, to love it, to become a part of it, to appreciate the discoveries made along the journey, and not to be focused on results. It is essential to enjoy and appreciate the process and not to be focused only on the goal. By not focusing on an expected result, the potential rewards become limitless! Each person will experience what is in their best interest and for their well-being. It is equally important to exercise a sense of humor on this journey and to keep laughing at the funny things that happen along the way.

There is a beginning to this process, but there is no end. It will be ongoing, even after *YOUR* dream relationship has come true.

IT IS A WAY OF LIFE — IT IS A LIFE'S WORK!

You might think while reading this, "Yes, this is fine if you are single and want to create a relationship, but what about me? I'm in a relationship and want to improve it." The same process applies to you, dear friend. For example, if you realize that you are in a treadmill relationship and want to create *YOUR* dream relationship—DO IT! It is a choice and we need to remember that on an essence level we are responsible only for ourselves.

Before starting the eleven-step process, imagine blowing the outcome—your dream relationship—into a beautiful, rainbow-colored, imaginary bubble and then releasing it to fly free and merge with the universal flow of things. This means letting go of the outcome, letting go of thoughts like, "Will my current partner join the process and when?" "Will he/she be my dream partner?" "Will we have to separate?" etc. The focus on the process is important; the rest will be taken care of by the innerself, who knows best. The "healing" of a relationship can be a coming together or a going apart. As we go through the eleven-step process and meet the innerself, trusting it to guide us, we will know and understand that, whatever the outcome, it will be for our highest good.

Let's begin the journey—eleven steps to the pinnacle of the triangle, to the place of unconditional love, to peace, ecstasy, bliss and the knowing of timelessness and dimensionlessness—

YOUR DREAM RELATIONSHIP

ELEVEN STEPS TO
Your Dream Relationship

These eleven steps are based on our experiences that led to our actualized dream relationship. These steps are intended as tools for you to use, *only if you decide to do so,* in creating your own personal path to a dream relationship.

A well-maintained body will be a comfortable "temple" in which we can meet and experience our various life choices.

Physical Exercise

Exercise is a means to enhance our life choices and not an end in itself. Exercise trains and develops the body through systematic practice while preparing it for use in all of life's activities. For example, a pianist may do finger exercises to play the piano.

We found it valuable to play the role of an architect and to begin building an exercise program by outlining all of our ideas on a piece of paper. We've intentionally chosen the words "exercise program" to make certain that exercise is understood as a process. Next, we narrowed down the ideas to those we would definitely commit to doing. We added to the list all the things we would need (apparatus, clothing, time frame, etc.) Then we moved from the role of architect to that of general contractor and made that list a reality by assembling all the tools and personal assistance required. The time came to become the

---

We suggest that you consult with a medical expert
prior to choosing or beginning your exercise program.

laborer and "Do it!" As the laborer, we sometimes found the general contractor's choice of tools needed changes, or that the architect's approach needed modification. Changes are generally required along the way to facilitate growth, so we made the necessary adjustments to improve the process of our program.

The following suggestions are offered as something to consider while designing a physical exercise program:

1. Consult with a medical expert prior to choosing or beginning an exercise program.

2. Consider a program that benefits the whole body and that emphasizes breathing and coordination.

3. Look carefully at your current life style and design a program that will work within it. For example, if you travel a great deal, the choice needs to be available during your travels. If your current life style is full of activity, it may require rescheduling and/or eliminating some existing activities.

4. *Begin whatever program you've designed with the affirmation, "I commit to doing it regularly."* We have found it most helpful to repeat the exercise program at least four times per week.

5. Begin slowly; there is no hurry, no finish line. This is a process, not a competition. It is only important to *continue*! Exercise in itself may not be enjoyable, but this hard work has its just rewards, *e.g.*, reduced stress level, increased energy, improved strength and endurance, healthier complexion, sense of accomplishment and mind clarity. There will be days when creative reasons run wild, tempting and

baiting us to avoid our regular exercise program. At this time, we need to strengthen our *commitment* and allow the memories of past rewards from exercising to act as motivation. Creative excuses can easily lead to avoidance.

6. Find a time that will be available every day. One method is to exercise the first thing after waking up. This ensures that it will be done and will have the body's motor purring along with a sense of accomplishment to start the day.

7. Stay with whatever time is chosen. There will be days when excuses flourish as to why the exercise should be skipped. We found it valuable to brush those excuses gently aside, to begin the routine and to affirm it as a valued priority in our daily life choices.

Many of us carry out an extensive maintenance program on our homes, cars and so on to ensure that they last a long time, look appealing and function well. Our exercise program is intended to help do the same for our body. When our car is well-maintained, we sit in it with a comfortable feeling, knowing it will start and carry us to our destination with ease. A well-maintained body will be a comfortable "temple" in which we can meet and experience our various life choices.

A well-rounded exercise program uses all of our physical parts and helps us to remain strong, clean and vital. An exercise program acts as a cleansing agent, helping the body to get rid of unwanted waste. Each day we load the body with things that eventually become waste products. These wastes are the result of food, drink, thought, stress, experiences and so on. This ongoing waste-loading requires a maintenance program that will ensure its elimination. A regular exercise program is just the ticket.

Remember that maintenance does not mean overindulging in an exercise program. We are attempting to reach an appropriate balance. REST is an important part of a balanced exercise program because it refreshes, restores and energizes our body and our sense of well-being. It also helps to bring peace, to offer relief from distressing, annoying and tiring occurrences and to calm our physical, mental and emotional bodies. Determining what is best for our ever-changing life styles is a process of self-observation, experimentation and adjustment. It will be helpful to look at the following areas, as well as others considered applicable, to determine our own appropriate rest requirements: (1) *Sleep* is our naturally recurring form of rest during which we experience little conscious thought or voluntary movement; (2) *Quiet Time* is our time spent alone, calm and absent of motion; (3) *In-Between Time* is the time spent gaining some relaxing moments between our various activities.

Too often we hear that physical exercise is given credit for benefitting only the physical body (weight, shape, complexion, muscle tone). We have clearly experienced additional benefits for the emotional body (less anxiety, less stress), the mental body (more clarity, improved memory), and the spiritual body (more frequent recognition of something greater to help keep things in perspective).

A multitude of benefits awaits to be realized. It takes commitment and effort to experience them.

EXAMPLE (ALIX). The stormy waters of my second failed marriage had calmed and I had settled into my new home. Then I made the important decision to start an exercise program. The apartment complex had a swimming pool. Please understand that I'm not especially fond of swimming, but I swam every morning before going to work for at least a half hour. It was a tough discipline, but very rewarding. I felt strong and alive every morning after this workout. A sense of accomplishment engulfed me by the time I reached my office.

In addition, I decided to resume yoga exercises for an hour and a half upon arriving home from work. The breathing, relaxation, concentration, postures, gentle stretching and balancing of the yoga exercises allowed me to let go of the tensions and stresses of the day.

I later changed the aerobic swimming to riding an exercise bike. The bike was on the outside deck of my apartment and gave me the advantage of being outside rather than inside.

This balanced exercise program, after I overcame the initial hardships, gave me a sense of well-being. I looked forward to doing it. It truly became a part of me.

EXAMPLE (RONALD). While living in San Francisco, I spent some of my free time walking the beaches along the ocean. One day a young man ran by and I decided to do a little running. Well, what a shock to my body and ego. I could barely run twenty-five yards before stopping completely out of breath. I looked up and down the beach and decided that I would begin jogging and walking about three miles until I could jog the entire distance without stopping. The next morning I headed to the beach to begin my challenge. I showed up seven days a week, with the soft sand, fog, rain, wind and those beautiful sunrise mornings with the ocean waves crashing to the shore as the birds danced to morning's music. Jog, walk, jog, walk. . . . After two months, I completed this distance without a stop. Wherever you lived, you probably heard my scream of joy.

During this time, my weight fell from one hundred and eighty pounds to one hundred and sixty-five pounds, my complexion was rosy, and I was feeling and thinking more clearly.

Jogging became an important part of my life. It was portable and consequently easy to do while traveling. There were so many mornings when I would awaken and find so many different reasons not to jog, and then my heart would remind me of how wonderful I felt after completing the run. The reward of feeling strong, alert and vital was too great to miss.

A friend suggested joining a yoga class. The class consisted of a half hour of breathing, a half hour of meditation and one hour of yoga exercises. The yoga exercises made me aware of how constricted my body was. I could not touch my toes with my knees straight. My hands reached to just below my knees. Yoga was not totally compatible with running. Running was tightening my muscles while yoga was stretching and loosening them. However, running was still important to me and I accepted the limitations it put on my yoga.

STEP 2

*Let's allow our body to guide us
to our appropriate diet.*

Diet

Our regular exercise program needs to be accompanied by an appropriate diet. To us, the word diet means "a way of life in which we decide what is appropriate for us to eat and drink." Each person has a slightly different body and each different body has a separate set of requirements. The purpose of this step is to discover our own specific requirements.

In today's world, the mass media constantly promotes products to make us look, feel and perform better by eating a certain food, drinking a particular beverage, ingesting something or looking like some chiseled Greek model. Nature hardly intended for approximately all six billion of us to look the same or to eat and drink the same thing at the same time. Nature creates all things slightly differently. These differences include preferences dependent upon availability, quality, quantity, individual needs and other factors. This variety of conditions disperses consumption, enabling nature to replenish what has

---

We suggest that you consult with a dietary expert
prior to designing your appropriate diet.

been consumed. Nature has an innate way of balancing. By taking individual responsibility for determining our specific dietary needs, we honor and obey nature's beneficial ways.

It is important to read books/magazines and ask questions of reliable people about the subject of nutrition and food preparation. These consultants may include: doctors, health food store proprietors, educators on nutrition, chefs, schools, dietitians at hospitals and others you feel guided to ask. We generally take time to consider what we hear/read and decide if we think and feel it is appropriate for us. We choose sources that inspire our interests and motivate us to act.

Let's start with a dietary practice that speaks to the greatest part of our physical make up—WATER. Each of us is about ninety-five percent water as an infant and about seventy percent water as an aging adult. The importance of replenishing the physical body with water can't be emphasized enough. Drinking about eight glasses of pure water per day (bottled or from a purification system) will assist in cleansing the body while maintaining the required balance of this most essential need. It is a relatively simple practice: drink water and feel the difference!

Next, exercise will most likely bring about a change in the foods we select. As our body is strengthened and brought into action, its requirements may change. The body may say it needs more water and/or fresh vegetables, and it may demand fewer sweets and fats. A tired, unexercised body remains slow, listless and apathetic to the point of foregoing the importance of sending messages concerning the body's needs. This type of body asks nothing and tells us nothing. On the other hand, a well-exercised body asks for its needs to be met and alerts us to developing problems.

It takes time to learn which foods help or hinder our personal sense of well-being. Some of the most beneficial foods are fresh, whole fruits, vegetables, grains and legumes. With the assistance of our regular exercise and appropriate water consumption, we may identify and eliminate items that we know aren't healthy and which make us tired, irritable and/or confused. We need to be careful not to be swayed by what others have told us is satisfying for them or taking that as meaningful to us. It is important to practice differentiating between what our body tells us and what others have told us. It is a trial-and-error process. For example, women during pregnancy often ask for foods that they never thought of asking for while not pregnant. Sometimes we get a craving for carrots that wasn't stimulated by an outside message. These are examples of the body asking us to supply a need. In Step Three—Freeing Yourself From Drugs, Alcohol and Tobacco—we further discuss how our actions can throw out-of-kilter the body's important function of asking/telling us what it needs.

Along the way, we have experimented with our diet, fine-tuned it and adjusted it to our forever-changing bodies. An experiment we use is to eliminate a particular food for a month. During this time we discover whether we experience any noticeable differences. If we feel better and more energized, we continue without the food and then try eliminating another. This process teaches what effect eating or not eating certain foods has on our sense of well-being. It continues to offer us reliable, first-hand results regarding our personal needs, while keeping us attentive to maintaining an energizing and beneficial diet.

Finally, *it is necessary to establish a food intake based on common sense and to make an effort to acquire knowledge about it. We may be surprised at how well we can manage an appropriate diet. There is no end in dieting; it is an ongoing process.*

Digestion is a strenuous and energy-consuming activity. In Western culture, eating and digesting have ironically become a form of "exercise." We observe the Western, sedentary, average daily life style to be: sleeping eight hours, sitting eight hours at work, riding one hour in a car, eating two hours, watching TV for three hours and doing two hours of miscellaneous chores. All this "sitting around" results in an excess of energy that constantly asks to be utilized. Instead of a moving physical exercise, we grab a snack while at one of the "sitting places" and the exercise of digestion begins. This additional digestion process (overeating) creates the feeling of being tired while increasing the load of waste in the body. All this "sitting" forces the body's important parts to ignore and forget their roles. The old saying is, "If you don't use it, you lose it." We have noticed that not using the body physically and not nourishing it appropriately causes it to become dysfunctional and diseased (dis-ease: not at ease; uncomfortable). It is important to recognize when the body needs food for energy and when it is being overfed with that Western-culture form of exercise, "digestion."

Each of us has individual and changing requirements for food intake, digestion, absorption and use. We need to take a committed approach but also allow ourselves to be flexible. Our days of faltering become great reminders of why we've attentively chosen our appropriate diet.

Let's allow our body to guide us to our appropriate diet!

EXAMPLE (ALIX). For eight months I had followed a very strict diet of fruit, vegetables and water. In the morning I had fresh-squeezed orange juice, at lunch a pound of fresh fruit (in season), for dinner fresh or steamed vegetables, and at least eight glasses of water, but never with meals. This strict diet had two dramatic results: (1) a clear mind with an enormous amount of energy—never feeling tired, never feeling better; (2) weight loss. I'm five feet, seven inches tall, and my weight fell from one hundred twenty pounds to one hundred pounds. This was of concern to me. I chose a middle-of-the-road diet by adding cereals, legumes, grains and cheese. My weight reached my comfort level; however, my energy and mind clarity never reached those ecstatic levels of the original diet.

Later I went through some periods of eating meat, poultry and fish. My food combining was not always in the best interest of easy and proper digestion. This fall-back from the original, elevating diet resulted in poorer complexion, more body odors, less energy and less clarity of thought. After experimenting, I chose a balanced diet with plenty of pure water, fruit, vegetables, cereals, grains, legumes, cheese, yogurt and an occasional sweet treat, poultry or fish.

EXAMPLE (RONALD). Shortly after my exercise program had become regular, my desire for certain foods changed. I ate fewer and fewer heavy foods, such as meat, dairy products and sweets. Fresh fruits, vegetables and water became my staple.

Reading about recommended dietary requirements, which had always been of interest, led me to experiment and eliminate certain foods or food groups from my diet. Butter and bread were two foods that added weight to me regardless of my exercise program. A solid aerobic exercise controlled my sweets intake. At first I consciously stopped eating all meat, fish and poultry. It hurt me deeply to realize how unnecessary and cruel it was to kill animals. In fact, I felt stronger, more energized and lighter without eating animal parts. After a time of experimenting, I chose a balanced diet very similar to the one Alix mentioned in her example.

STEP 3

*Let's honor the body,
that sacred temple, with loving,
considerate and appropriate behavior.*

Freeing Yourself From Drugs, Alcohol & Tobacco

The preceding steps all asked for change. Well, Step Three also asks for change. We'd like to re-emphasize that our eleven-step process requires a continuing effort and commitment in order to achieve a sense of well-being, happiness, clarity of thought, inner peace, self-confidence and other beneficial attributes. The focus needs to be kept on the process, not the outcome! This process is a tool to be used in the most exciting endeavor available to humankind—creation, the creation of self by the very innerself. Many times we get trapped in the behavioral patterns of addiction, self-abuse and denial. These often prevent us from recognizing and/or remembering how wonderful life is without them. When we operate in these types of patterns it becomes a rapid-turning circle that prohibits anything else from entering. This step is about bringing our life into a process where we recognize and let go of destructive, self-limiting patterns and begin to welcome and accept new, healthy and self-expanding adventures.

We've limited this section to three representative categories—drugs, alcohol and tobacco—and will refer to any or all of them as "item(s)." It is important to understand that occasional use of these items under certain circumstances is not what we're suggesting be changed. For example, there may be a time when you and your chosen medical expert decide on a particular drug for your use. We suggest that the decision of when to use or not to use them be made from the innerself. That is the key throughout our process, to decide from within. Each step in this eleven-step process promotes an opening of communication with the innerself.

The choice to introduce any of these items (drugs, alcohol, and/or tobacco) into the body may indicate a conflict between an outer-created self and a smothered innerself. By using these self-limiting items, we attempt to escape the uncomfortable feeling about the outer world and touch the world of the innerself. With the first use of the item, we are *misled* into believing that it has touched the innerself, slightly, but enough to try the item again. The feeling of being freed from the outer world is experienced because of this introduction of the item into the body. While it makes us feel separated from our outer world by blocking and numbing our human faculties, it also forces a separation between us and our body. Where does this leave us? Lost and in limbo between the outer world and the inner world.

The item inhibits the physical body from operating in a natural and efficient manner. All these items either speed the body up or slow it down, above or below an acceptable mode of operation. After the item's initial effect disappears, the body is tired, out-of-sorts and many times exhausted. Our outer choices forced the body to behave in ways that were unnatural. The item caused one of the most amazing processes in this world, the functioning of the human body, to be abusively altered. The body, through the innerself, makes choices to keep its magnificence intact. Choosing an item from outer-world information and literally forcing it upon the body is very harsh treatment to give to a sacred temple. The body is the most relevant vehicle for the human experience; as such, it requires reverent care.

Each time we reintroduce an item with increasing frequency, the body closes down further to avoid being forced upon by something it didn't request. Ingesting these items is a form of oppression and a rape of the body at the same time. The outer self's decision to use the item without agreement from the body is a form of oppression and the foreign item's entry mounts an attack on the body, raping it of its natural free will. The body's defense of closing down to protect itself from the item is countered by the outer self with a larger and larger dose in an attempt to regain that feeling of the first experience. The body, to protect itself, resists the item by closing down further and further. This closing down lessens the intended perceived experience while driving the outer self further apart from the body. It becomes a war: the outer self bombards the body with larger doses and the body constricts and retreats. After each experience, the shell-shocked body takes a little longer to regain a semblance of normality. As the pauses between doses become shorter and shorter, the body tends to remain withdrawn and to forego any attempt to return to its natural state. If the use of the items continues and/or escalates, a point is reached where the outer self becomes so confused that the act becomes a habit. The physical body deteriorates quickly due to this unnatural state of constriction and withdrawal, remaining hidden and frustrated from the lost opportunity to correct the situation. The body is constantly under a smothering attack and never has time to clear the previous dose. A build-up of the doses takes place in the physical body and weakens it to the point of complete surrender.

Allow this description to act as a warning as to how outer-directed behavior can violate one of our most precious gifts, the body. Let's honor the body, that sacred temple, with loving, considerate and appropriate behavior.

The habitual use of these items is a reflection of today's outer world: they are convenient and immediate—just the prescription for addiction. This combination doesn't leave time for self-consideration and self-evaluation. Addiction manifests as a form of enslavement that controls and diminishes a person's ability to think and participate in life's activities. The more we use the item, the more we are being controlled.

Society validates using these items by emphasizing "how many people are using them." Our senses are inundated with messages that either directly or indirectly ask for participation. These messages come at us from TV, radio, music, movies, magazine/newspaper articles, books, advertising, word of mouth, rumor, friends, acquaintances and so on. When one or several of our senses are stimulated by any or all of the afore-mentioned messages, they ask us to do something, sometime and somewhere. The more frequent the same message, the more it is reinforced in our brain, and the more it agitates our mind until we act on the message.

By listening to the demands or enticements of others to use these items and then by acting on these messages, we sacrifice the body for the sake of the outer message. These messages are not speaking to the body, nor to that place of inner knowing that resides in the heart, the innerself. Why? The innerself would never allow these items into its "temple." *The body is a magnificent, amazing, natural, free-flowing group of highly specialized and integrated, cooperative systems, enjoined to provide us with a clear and unencumbered sanctuary in which to experience life.* Let's honor our body as a marvelous gift while allowing it to communicate and guide us to what is best for us.

The body is so amazing and resilient. No matter how much we abuse it, recovery is always a welcome possibility. When we take action in agreement with the body, it responds with love and appreciation. It foregoes past differences in favor of new and agreeable beginnings.

Some of us have the discipline to develop on our own a program that eliminates the item(s) from our life. However, this is most often the exception.

Most people may need to consult with an assistance program that meets their needs and comfort level in order to work through this most difficult challenge. Being aware that we need to change and then taking the action of standing up for ourselves by *asking* for help, are very significant and rewarding steps. They are a very important beginning to overcoming addiction, self-abuse and denial.

So, to those of us who will do it and to those who have done it, CONGRATULATIONS!!!

For assistance, you might contact local or personal medical experts, hospital and/or local support groups. The local newspaper and the telephone book's yellow pages generally have listings and your local library should also have information about them. Some are funded by donations and may not require a fee. If you don't find a listing for your specific need, call one of the listed groups and *ask* for their help in finding your appropriate group.

EXAMPLE (ALIX). I had never smoked, drank about a glass of wine twice a month, and used over-the-counter and/or prescription drugs only in times of illness. When I got fully involved in my exercise program and balanced diet, that little bit of alcohol felt like an unnecessary burden to my system. I drank alcohol to be a part of the "group" at a party or business lunch. It was an outer-directed choice because I really never enjoyed the taste nor the feeling it gave me. I realized that it was time to be my innerself and that I didn't need alcohol at any time, no matter what the occasion.

EXAMPLE (RONALD). Being a person of play, tobacco, drugs and alcohol all were a part of my life at various times. Tobacco was the first to go. While sitting on a beach reading the Surgeon General's Warning about the dangers of smoking, my heart gave a yell, "Listen and stop this ridiculous habit." My mind agreed that research, time, money and human expertise were spent to protect me and that it was time to take this sound advice. I tossed the package of cigarettes away. That was the last of my tobacco smoking.

I began drinking alcohol as a senior in high school and it was not a pretty picture. Often I overindulged and became argumentative and neglectful of others and myself. At the age of twenty-four I experimented with marijuana and quit alcohol. Later, while working for a major corporation where alcohol was the accepted and expected social behavior, I began to drink again. I found that my argumentative nature was behind me, but my tendency to overindulgence was not.

When I started my regular exercise program and balanced diet, I quit alcohol and marijuana because they brought me down with a feeling of heaviness. Some people in my business and social circles were uneasy about my non-indulgence. I accepted their habits, but they were uncomfortable with my change.

I had used alcohol and drugs to be a part of the outer-world game. I was avoiding being my innerself. My alcohol and drug experiences numbed me into ignoring the inner plea to stop. As the inside gradually opened and replaced the outer image, discontinuing drugs and alcohol was very easy. My mind grew into agreement with the innerself.

*Having sexual experiences
before self-discovery is like putting the cart
before the horse and never realizing
that it is "bass aackwards."*

Celibacy *(Temporarily!)*

Celibacy is a word you probably didn't want to hear. The good news is that it is suggested only as a temporary experience.

We found that celibacy enabled us to use our life-force energy more consciously. Our view is that one energy animates each human being, the life-force energy. We realized that we give the one life-force energy several different names, depending how we use it, *e.g.*, sexual energy, creative energy, physical energy. We receive only a certain amount of energy and each of us determines how it will be used. For example, if the total amount of energy received equals one hundred percent, we may use forty percent for our daily physical activities including our biological needs, twenty percent for our emotional needs, thirty percent for our sexual activity and ten percent for our creativity (the unencumbered expression of the innerself). Our use of celibacy is intended to make certain that our creative (innerself) experiences are increased and that sexual experiences are kept to a basic minimum. *Celibacy is a method to redistribute our supply of life-force energy.* As we reduced our use of sexual energy, we found our creative approaches to life's challenges became much more powerful.

Sexual energy, a powerful part of the life-force energy, is intended as the energy of procreation. When sexual energy is used excessively, just to satisfy sensual pleasure, it doesn't fulfill its intended purpose and thus upsets the important balance of the life-force energy. In this case, much of the life-force energy expresses through a lower energy center and may never reach the other centers to ensure harmony and balance of the physical, mental, emotional and spiritual bodies. Various traditions have recognized seven major energy centers, also known as *chakras.* These are: (1) root, at the base of the spine; (2) abdominal, at the navel; (3) solar plexus; (4) heart; (5) throat; (6) third eye, at the center of the forehead; and (7) crown, at the top of the head.

At times and for various reasons we may refrain from using our sexual energy even though we disagree with the reason. In these cases, the build-up of self-induced, unexpressed sexual energy can take place, resulting in an explosion of misguided sexual expression. When sexual energy is repressed and controlled in order to conform to unagreeable outer messages, it may result in an imbalance in the physical, mental, emotional and spiritual bodies. *By acknowledging our powerful sexual energy, instead of using it exclusively for sensual pleasure, or repressing and controlling it, we can learn to transmute it into creative energy by "creating a flow" from the lower energy centers to the higher ones.*

Take a moment to imagine part of the life-force energy being redirected from sexual energy to creative energy. This is an attempt to take from the abundance of life-force energy currently used as sexual energy and to make use of it as creative energy. It is not intended to eliminate the sexual energy, which is a duly-balanced portion of the life-force energy. We are moving toward a reasonable balance.

Whenever we've felt an excessive build-up of sexual energy, we've used the following exercise to assist in redistributing/transforming it to all seven major energy centers (chakras). You can do this exercise if it resonates with you and if you feel comfortable doing it.

EXERCISE
**Redistributing/Transforming Excessive Sexual Energy
to All Seven Major Energy Centers**

1. Sit or lie quietly in a position that allows the spine to remain
    in straight alignment. Close your eyes and breathe gently
    and deeply. The chosen position is not intended to promote
    sleep.

2. Quiet yourself and remain this way for a few minutes and
    accept, without judgment, your excessive sexual energy.

3. **Visualize the excessive sexual energy** entering a balloon
    at your sexual energy center (second chakra, abdomen) and
    accept that you are going to redistribute it to all seven major
    energy centers.

4. Slowly move the balloon to your root chakra (first chakra,
    at the base of the spine) and slowly release some of the
    energy from the balloon into the first chakra. Feel the
    energy merge with the first chakra and see the balloon
    getting smaller.

5. Slowly move the balloon up to the second chakra (abdo-
    men) and slowly release some of the energy from the
    balloon into the second chakra. Feel the energy merge with
    the second chakra and see the balloon getting smaller.

6. Slowly move the balloon up to the third chakra (solar
    plexus) and slowly release some of the energy from the
    balloon into the third chakra. Feel the energy merge with
    the third chakra and see the balloon getting smaller.

7. Slowly move the balloon up to the fourth chakra (heart) and slowly release some of the energy from the balloon into the fourth chakra. Feel the energy merge with the fourth chakra and see the balloon getting smaller.

8. Slowly move the balloon up to the fifth chakra (throat) and slowly release some of the energy from the balloon into the fifth chakra. Feel the energy merge with the fifth chakra and see the balloon getting smaller.

9. Slowly move the balloon up to the sixth chakra (between the eyebrows, third eye) and slowly release some of the energy from the balloon into the sixth chakra. Feel the energy merge with the sixth chakra and see the balloon getting smaller.

10. Slowly move the balloon up to the seventh chakra (top of the head, crown) and slowly release some of the energy from the balloon into the seventh chakra. Feel the energy merge with the seventh chakra. As this last bit of energy is released, imagine the balloon dissolving and returning to the universal flow of things.

11. Spend a few moments to feel the balance of the life-force energy in these seven energy centers. When you're ready, slowly become aware of your physical surroundings and then slowly open your eyes.

This is a great tool to use whenever you notice the energy in any one of the major energy centers becoming excessive to the point of distracting you from a current activity. For example, you might be writing an important letter when an excessive amount of sexual energy surfaces and prevents you from maintaining your full, undivided attention. Using the visualization can help.

We use a mini-version of this exercise to center and balance us when we are out and about, which consists of taking a few moments to close our eyes, visualizing the excessive energy and then seeing it redistributed/transformed to our seven major chakras.

Sometimes we never quite understand or recognize the potential consequences of our sexual behavior. For example, suppose we socialize at a local club and after a few drinks feel the need for sexual attention and find it conveniently in the person sitting next to us. Off we go for a night of sexual, sensual pleasures. It feels good and the next morning we are free to move on without any sense of responsibility. But, wait a moment! A week later we discover that we contracted a sexually-transmittable disease as a result of the one-night stand—bingo, the underlying consequence! *Celibacy gives us an opportunity to recognize and observe undesirable sexual behavior patterns when they arise and to change them in order to avoid the underlying consequences.*

Many people also misunderstand the underlying reasons for sexual attraction and for the misplaced preoccupation with the seeking of sexual stimulation. We've learned from the world outside and through experience that sexual stimulus leads to orgasm, which elevates us to a sense of bliss. We don't fully understand that there may be other excellent means of attaining such ecstasy or bliss. Being enamored with this blissful result removes us from the outer world. Then we attempt to regain this over and over and over again through sex. Through orgasm, we have reached a place that is totally who we are— absent of all else in the outer world. It feels magnificent. Then we return to our outside structure (sometimes slowly, sometimes abruptly). Many times we attribute this inner elevation to our sexual partner. The association is made—partner and bliss. This misappropriated status of the partner is an attempt to see him/her as being responsible for our bliss. If we don't feel our bliss, the partner is guilty by association and then accused of changing. This is a good time to pause and notice how some people, maybe you, look for sexual intimacy with another partner as an answer to a failing relationship. Many times, after a blissful orgasm is reached with a different partner, we say, "This one is different." It isn't. It is us again experiencing ourselves.

To us, *bliss is residing in the innerself,* which explains why this elevated state is not at all exclusive to the sexual act. We have found that we can reach a state of bliss and rapture through meditation, through lying in a meadow or sitting under a tree listening to the sound of nature, watching a beautiful sunset, being in the presence of someone with whom we have a deep connection on an essence level, and so on, through any experience that will trigger the merging with the innerself, our essence.

Notice how our body reacts to the different ways that trigger this blissful state. How do we feel after a sexual orgasm? An answer may be, "I feel tired; I want to sleep." How do we feel after having reached bliss through meditation or an experience in nature? If you have had such an experience, you know. If not, let us share our experience and encourage you to work toward it. We have had feelings of being energized and vitalized—just the opposite of feeling tired. Doesn't that in itself offer a clue?

Celibacy is a tough discipline to get through because of cultural training and past personal experiences. However, we feel it is essential, because it gives us needed time and energy to communicate with our innerself, while putting the outer world's bombardment of sexual messages on hold.

There is an irony to the outer sexual message. We can't find what we're told exists. The media bombards us with sensual, sexual innuendoes. Sexual salespersonship runs rampant in Western culture and persuades us to believe, "It turns us on." It really turns on the outer self and we buy the game, and thus we sell out the innerself. Yet let's look at our lives and count the times we've actually experienced the media's suggestive portrayals. Not often, if at all. The advertised sexual experience isn't a natural event. It is scripted, staged, musically scored, acted and edited to bait us into believing. Once we believe, we assume that everyone believes, but, to our astonishment, this is not quite true. Our desperate search for someone to act out this advertisement continues. We may even find an agreeable partner, only to discover that the conversation is awkward, the setting is much more sparse, the partner doesn't look like, sound like or sing like the ad, and our buoyed expectations last only as long as the ad, about thirty seconds. When the outer world controls our sexual experiences, perceived or real, we may have sold out our inner sexuality, our innerself.

Having sexual experiences before self-discovery is like putting the cart before the horse and never realizing that it is "bass aackwards." Being sexually active while trying to discover an inner dream relationship adds confusion and certainly delays self-discovery.

Sexual intimacy is a part of a dream relationship, but, to what degree, should be decided by the innerself. Let's not try now, while going through this step, to figure out what it will or would be like with our future dream partner, rather, just stay in the now, in the process, and celibacy is part of that process. The innerself will show us ways that cannot be realized now. This is an evolving process, an unfolding of the innerself.

EXAMPLE (ALIX). After having left two short, failed marriages, I looked for the pattern that was causing these failures. Before each marriage, I had a "gut feeling" of hesitation, that something wasn't right, but my mind had reasons to enter into those marriages. Later I discovered those mind reasons were not in agreement with my innerself.

Celibacy was a choice to keep me from getting intimately involved while I focused on myself. There was no partner to expect from, give to, or receive from. *During celibacy I gave myself attention, love, acceptance and forgiveness, while receiving an inner knowing and happiness.* Yes, I definitely learned that happiness is inherent to my nature; it is there all the time, and nobody outside creates it for me.

About a year after my parents died, I thought about a relationship and almost frantically pushed toward one, even paying a fee to a marriage agency to get in touch with prospective partners. The agency sent two men and, after several hours of conversation with each of them, it was most apparent that I wasn't ready. I had given in to a sudden feeling of loneliness and anxiousness and was attempting to rush through my celibacy rather than to make the most of the process. This was my reoccurring pattern of impatience, an urgent need to do something now. This time I felt protected by an invisible force telling me to continue my celibacy, an inward journey of self-discovery.

EXAMPLE (RONALD). I had experienced many failed relationships. There was definitely some inherent flaw in my methods. Celibacy seemed to be a good place to start a change, since most of my relationships began with a sexual experience. It felt strange, not being involved sexually with someone. I didn't announce my celibacy to friends, but they saw a change in my ways. I was no longer chasing skirts and dating. Remaining celibate was a firm decision. Thoughts came over me like, "Will I ever be sexually intimate with a woman again? If so, when?" along with many other outer-directed mind questions. This sudden change to being celibate was a shock to my outer image, and my mind tried desperately to persuade me to continue as I had been previously. However, that little voice inside asked me to step back and observe the temptation, to recognize the similarities of past failures, and to take my time and be patient in learning about myself. I had a couple of flings along the way, but they were occasional and I recognized them as such.

During celibacy, slowly it became clear how the outer world's frequent sexual messages, along with my self-image and resulting expectations, were smothering me from noticing other choices. I experienced a frustrating cycle that ended with the same repeated discoveries of failure. Celibacy was a time to live without being influenced by the outer-directed, fictitious sexual messages and to discover choices in agreement with my innerself.

STEP 5

*Inside there is a wisdom
to be heard.*

Quieting Your Mind

Quieting Your Mind sounds rather simple, but remains a most difficult challenge, especially in our fast-paced society. You may ask, "Why is it so important to quiet my mind?" A silent mind is "a highway" to the innerself. The innerself, that formless, dimensionless flow of energy, that we cannot see, that has no weight and yet exists, can only be reached when our internal chatter-box—our mind—grows pure and silent through deep absorption. In the space between thoughts, we find the innerself. We get to that "highway" through discipline and practice.

First, we have to recognize why our mind is such a chatter-box, why it maintains its continuous internal dialogue. For example: "If I decide to go and see Jo, I had better be prepared; I had better finish this task first. But if I finish this first, I might be late, and that could upset Jo. Or maybe I could do the errand on my way over to Jo's, or perhaps I should take a taxi instead of driving. It would be ridiculous to pay for a taxi when I can drive, and what would Jo think if I arrived in a taxi?"—and on

29

and on. This chatter-box is a result of our belief systems. We call it the *domestication* of the mind, the imprinting that we receive from parents, relatives, schoolmates, teachers, friends, radio, television, books, magazines and so on, all who have made their contribution. It starts at conception and continues throughout life. The mind is continuously stimulated to respond and wander. Our socially-approved belief systems tell us who we are, how we are, how we will be, how to react, and these slowly build an outside image of us that our mind accepts and then constantly keeps reminding us of through the eternal chatter. *It is important to know that our chatter-box, our mind, is not us and that the outside image is not us. What we truly are and need is inside, in those spaces between thoughts. Inner knowledge is there to be explored, discovered, listened to and acted upon.*

SILENCE is the discipline to get to that inner place and also an effective way to shut down the chatter-box. It is very important to start practicing silence by making room every day for quiet time, if only for a few minutes. Our fast-paced life style needs to be balanced with silence.

During your quiet time, you may begin by using an affirmation or prayer that will focus your mind only on this one thought; then repeat the affirmation or prayer over and over again to reduce the chatter. You may notice that other thoughts will come up and distract you from your affirmation or prayer. Gently brush them away and return to your original focus. You can practice this exercise several times a day, anytime, anywhere. You need not sit in a special posture or in a special place.

Another suggestion for Quieting Your Mind is meditation (quiet time). It will be important to remain awake during meditation and to sit or lie in a position that provides straight alignment for your spine. Lying down may promote sleep, but this is not the intent. You may find that soft music (without lyrics) will add to your quietness or help screen out distracting noises. Choose a comfortable place and a time that will keep you away from outside disturbances. In the beginning it will be difficult, with hundreds of thoughts that attempt to keep you involved in the mind's chatter. Gently brush those thoughts away without becoming discouraged or upset. After practicing meditation for a while at the same time and place each day, it will become easier and easier to let go of thoughts, to open up and to get glimpses of the innerself.

You may find that the best way of Quieting Your Mind is not through sitting in meditation, but through contemplation of pleasant occurrences in nature, or through walking, running or whatever. There is no blueprint. You create your own, and that will be your appropriate method of getting to the "highway" that leads to your innerself. Whatever you do to quiet your mind, remember you've made a great start!

Over time, you may *try* to eliminate all outer thoughts (very difficult). Try this exercise: count slowly from one to ten and then back from ten to one. On the inhalation hear "one" and on the exhalation, "two"—slowly and gently. During this time, you may hear yourself again interrupted by words, thoughts, remembrances and ideas from your outer world. Accept those without challenge and gently brush them away, returning to the number counting. We have experienced that SILENCE means discarding the outer-world thoughts, the mind's chatter, and that it leads to discovering the inner voice.

As we get beyond our mind's chatter, reaching the innerself, we may be surprised at our experiences. They won't have anything to do anymore with the "realities" of our chatter-box. We just are—OURSELVES. We need to learn not to question those inner experiences, but simply to acknowledge them, accept them, trust them and cherish them for what they are—US, the inner truth.

This truth voices itself most often in a very subtle way and it can speak at any time, not just during our "quiet time." We can have our greatest "insights" while taking a shower (the water tends to harmonize our frequency with our "inner flow"), or when our body and mind function as if on "automatic pilot," such as when we do some type of activity that doesn't require our full mental concentration, like washing dishes, sweeping the floor, weeding the garden, or the like. On those occasions we sometimes happen to just BE, while our mind goes blank for a few moments. And then, suddenly, *without* thinking about something in particular, we get the greatest idea, insight, answer or prompting, like a flash. What has happened? We have touched the space between thoughts, the all-knowing infinite self; the innerself is communicating. So, let's be aware of that very subtle communication, let's honor and respect this truth, which may voice itself more and more frequently as we advance on our "highway." We'll find a new and real "innerself-confidence."

Self-confidence is often a very misused word because it is used to describe "only" the outer self, while ignoring the innerself. The mind is trained by others to experience what is outside. This creates a dualistic relationship between what is inside (being left undiscovered) and what is outside (which we are taught to discover). Life is led primarily on the outside, yet inside there is a wisdom to be heard. Most often the inside is denied, ignored and discredited by opposing outside actions. It is important to trust our innerself. We truly are our own best friend.

Quieting Your Mind is an exercise of silencing the chatterbox in order to hear your inner truth and knowledge. This process reveals, ever so slowly, the innerself that has been there all along. In time, the voice of the innerself may replace the disagreeable outer influences. There is no hurry in this step. Continue at a pace that is comfortable to you. Welcome and enjoy learning about yourself. Honor it. This is truly an everlasting friendship.

EXAMPLE (ALIX). My yoga program gave me an opportunity every day to practice quieting my mind. Many days it was impossible to stop my mind's chatter, because hundreds of outer-world thoughts came up. I gently brushed them away. Some days I went beyond the mind's chatter and experienced sounds, colors, words, feelings and images in a state of inner peace. I learned not to question those inner experiences, but to accept and cherish them as a part of me.

Being out in nature has always been a powerful way for me to quiet my mind and to take notice of my innerself. Lying in a meadow, sitting under a tree, looking at flowers or walking in a forest often triggered a feeling of merging with my surroundings, of bypassing my mind and joining directly with my innerself. The trees, flowers, grass and animals have always been dear friends—I talked to them and they talked to me. . . .

EXAMPLE (RONALD). In my first yoga class, I asked what to do during meditation. It was suggested that counting from one to ten and back to one (described above) might be of help. During the half hour, I got as far as four, one time. All other times, my chatter-box interceded. I was astonished at how difficult this simple exercise was for me and how easily distracted I was by events that were not of the present moment. I could not stay in the moment to the count of ten. Yoga classes provided me with a time to unwind, to quiet my active mind, and to feel myself. These experiences gradually helped shift my attention from the outer chatter to my inner voice.

If we have an open heart,
we will be like a tree rooted in the infinite
flow of knowing, wisdom and unconditional
love, which will undoubtedly bear fruit
when it is ready.

Opening Your Heart

Opening Your Heart is growing beyond the illusions and limitations of the mind and the senses, growing beyond the three-dimensional, the tangible, and reconnecting with that place of unconditional love that is within each and every one of us, the dimensionless INNERSELF. It means listening to the voice of the inner truth. Opening Your Heart is about relinquishing doubt and establishing an unconditional trust in the inner guidance. It also means accepting and enjoying our life experiences as they are. If we have an open heart, we will be like a tree rooted in the infinite flow of knowing, wisdom and unconditional love, which will undoubtedly bear fruit when it is ready.

Western culture places a huge emphasis on living a life based on the five sensory perceptions. The following is an example of how distortedly we can perceive a particular situation through our five senses. Science has discovered that our planet earth rotates on its axis and around the sun at an incredible speed. Yet our senses on which we rely so heavily don't see, hear, feel, taste or smell this speed. The mind often is compelled to give a name to sensory perceptions. When we are presented with something that goes beyond the tangible, our five senses become inadequate to provide the mind with information. We need to find alternative ways of perceiving and accepting those experiences.

An open heart accepts that there is a multitude of realms to be experienced, realms for which our mind doesn't have names. We may or may not have had an experience that we recognize as being in the metaphysical realm, an experience that puts humankind into perspective and allows us to recognize that there is much more than the outer (physical) self. Such an experience may have occurred while sitting under the stars at night, wondering, as a spiritual connection, a religious knowing, a vision of some future event, the hearing of a voice inside or as a gut feeling. We experienced something beyond our five senses, that is, the metaphysical.

The metaphysical reaches beyond our tangible body. It is important to learn how to expand our life to include perception of this valuable resource. We are like receivers with many different channels. Many times we limit the possibilities by repeatedly using the same, physical, channel. How do we discover the metaphysical and whether this is appropriate? We discover it through trial and error, as we have done for so long in the physical world.

The metaphysical is inner-driven and the physical is outer-driven. The inner driver has been used infrequently, if at all. Instead, we usually continue in the physical world by having others decide our experiments, absent of inner confirmation. We have trusted those outside, not trusted our innerselves, and thus avoided accepting responsibility for our actions. It is often uncomfortable to acknowledge this human shortcoming.

Most people have been overindulgent in the physical, and they need to achieve a balance by also using metaphysical resources. Many great masters on the earth, both of the physical and metaphysical persuasions, have emphasized what they understood best, and reminded us to integrate their messages in such a way as to attain a balance in life. We, as students of these masters, many times listen only to the primary teaching and ignore the message as a whole.

You may consider taking the time to read the books or listen to the teachings of various metaphysical teachers. Pay careful attention, for although their techniques may differ, the messages are the same; everything is ONE. When you hear something that resonates with your heart (not the mind—and this may take time to differentiate), incorporate it into your experiences and see if it works comfortably for you. You may find that it may take only one teacher or it may take several, but each will provide you with assistance in reaching balance.

Opening Your Heart means changing one's perceptions, relinquishing doubt and establishing an unconditional trust in the inner guidance. We need to trust and surrender to that invisible force, the dimensionless innerself, and to accept our life experiences as they are and for what they are—our lessons. The universe is not "out there to get us" and we are not its victims. It is there to help us learn. We need to know and trust that there are no mistakes in our life, that whatever happens to us happens for a purpose and teaches us. We may not understand each lesson or purpose at the time the experience occurs. It is helpful just to accept all events unconditionally, and the answer as to the "why" will certainly dawn on us when we are ready to grasp it. Let's remember that there is no right or wrong, there are only lessons. But don't we often strive to be right, to be perfect, forgetting in the meantime to be joyful and happy? Why are we choosing to be right instead of happy, when there is no right? Think about it.

Let's look at the heart as a symbol of life and living, of unconditional love and oneness. The physical heart opens and closes at a speed required to ensure balance while meeting the needs of the body. Our heart is a place where the merging and nourishment of the physical (blood) and the metaphysical (unconditional love) take place.

Unconditional love, the most important inherent property of the innerself, which resides in the heart, is simply the truth within each and every one of us. It harbors no purpose, no expectations, no obligations and no apologies. The journey of the eleven steps offers us an opportunity to experience this beautiful love and to bring it into every single facet of our daily life. Love is not an intellectual understanding. Love is beyond reason. It is a deep, heart-felt set of experiences.

LOVE IS ALL THERE IS!

With the assistance of unconditional love, our consciousness continues to move toward oneness. The major religions have long spoken of the oneness, and recently the science of quantum physics recognized that everything is interconnected—the unified field—oneness. Einstein acknowledged that his greatest insights came to him, not from what he had read or been taught, but from an unknown source. This conscious movement toward oneness needs to be accelerated on a micro-level in all of us.

If we open our heart and reconnect with our innerself, the unconditional love, the unity consciousness, we will know that the outer-created separateness is an illusion and that in fact our "physical" experiences are nothing but lessons for us to learn in order to get back to the oneness.

Opening Your Heart is a lifetime process with numerous plateaus along the way.

EXAMPLE (ALIX). The strong catapult into my transformation was the physical death of my parents in late 1985. They died seventeen days apart, having spent their last weeks in the same hospital room. Dad had been ill for two and a half years and Mom for eight months. Being the only child, the doctors had told me from the beginning that their illnesses were terminal.

Death became my greatest teacher. It taught me to be strong and stay in the moment, to live every day as if it would be the last and to always love my parents unconditionally. Death taught me to let go of all resentment and to forgive myself and my parents for any disagreements experienced during our life's journey.

In my quiet time, I sometimes felt the oneness and recognized that there would be no separation from the love between us. Those insights gave me tremendous support. My parents would make a transition into another realm. I was going to be alone, but I didn't feel victimized or a need to be pitied. I prayed to God that their suffering in the physical be ended, and that their spirits be set free. Later, during an emotion-clearing session with a professional, I realized that, on a very deep level, I had given them permission to leave. In turn, their leaving had given me the greatest gift of love, the freedom to discover and become who I truly am. It was a feeling of being freed from a lifetime of their expectations.

About two months after they had crossed over, I had a very ecstatic experience. During two and a half hours of reading and listening to classical music on a Sunday afternoon, I suddenly felt myself expanding with an enormous feeling of freedom that went through my whole being and moved towards the ceiling, filling the room. White and then golden light pulsated through my body. I didn't move for about fifteen minutes. Then my mind kicked in with the following guilt trip: "How can you have such an ecstatic feeling of freedom so soon after your parents' death?" My heart knew better—for it had opened. After this new beginning, there were periods when I lost track of my heart and became trapped in my outer-directed image, and I overindulged in buying sprees.

In 1986 I took an extended vacation to South America and again reconnected with my heart, especially at Machu Picchu in Peru, where I was literally energized. After five and a half weeks, I returned to my job and "saw a fog" covering my office. At that point, deep within, I knew that things had to change, when the time was right.

Another milestone on my inner journey occurred during a visit with a man I had met in Portugal. He shared with me his knowledge of metaphysical literature. This led me to books and experiences that furthered my awareness of the inner me.

EXAMPLE (RONALD). Play, play and more play best describes my life for the first twenty-seven years. I then got married and three years later was divorced. I felt like a complete failure and thought that all the world saw me that way. My heart broke open from the pain and made me extremely sensitive to everything in my life. I felt and recognized that people were assisting me, caring for me and loving me. At times I asked, "What is so different about me today, as opposed to a year ago?" I had opened my heart and was letting the inner me flow into the outer world. It was so simple being who and what I deeply felt. Successes seemed natural. Failures were clear and understood because I was now making choices from the inside.

Three months after accepting a job offer, the corporation where I worked closed its doors. Instead of being upset, I was concerned about my fellow employees and their families. The corporation offered me a job with another company under their umbrella, but my heart had already decided that I was moving to San Francisco. This job offer was the outer-directed world attempting to keep me from my inner knowing. The same lesson (job) was presented to me, just to see if I truly had learned the lesson. It came in a different package, fancier wrapping paper, bigger bow and more bells and whistles. My innerself prevailed and I moved on to the next lesson on my life's path.

During the next fifteen years in San Francisco, I slowly moved away from my innerself and again focused on my outer-directed image. I had achieved outer-driven success, but began to feel that something was missing. Through yoga practice I began to converse with the inner me. A friend from yoga class had just returned from a four-day retreat of silence. She said it was wonderful and that she had heard her true innerself. I knew at that moment, as appealing as it sounded, I was not ready to face the inner me. Why? Because I was living an outer-directed image that was in disagreement with my innerself.

Then, after ten and a half years with a certain corporation, I was fired without an explanation. My mind asked "why?" while my heart felt joy and freedom. Offers from the industry came and my mind pushed me to accept. However, my heart asked for time to breathe and live. I followed my heart. The home I had bought four years previously had been merely a stopover between my business travels. Now I spent weeks working in the yard, noticing a tree I hadn't seen before and asking, "How long have you been here?" Well, the tree had been there at least twenty-five years. My outer-directed, tread-mill life had kept me from noticing anything other than the outer-world assignments.

A friend called in May 1989 and asked me to pick up a book. She had suggested many books before, none of which I had read, but I did read this one. It talked about past-life regression, among other life experiences, and I read it non-stop. I called the author in July 1989 to ask for an appointment to do past-life regression sessions and was told it would be six months before I could be seen. A cancellation came up in September 1989 and, after four past-life regression sessions, I was joyously back in touch with the process of discovering my innerself. Opening my heart became a continuing process.

I learned to communicate with my innerself and rediscovered the little boy inside of me. He had stepped aside when I started listening to others. It was as if I had ignored him and now was reunited with him. I felt a great happiness in my heart to have the little boy return to ignite a wonderful sense of freedom and adventure. My heart had been numb and was now beating stronger while making me aware of what dwells inside.

*It is essential to face ourselves
with the "whole honest-to-God truth."
Let's not try to fool ourselves,
because we really can't.*

Facing Yourself

Facing Yourself is a journey in itself, again a journey from outward to inward. It is about recognizing who we are, through this following basic process:

1. Getting beyond our mistaken personality, which gets in the way of our real personality and prohibits it from doing its proper job, namely being the tool for our creation and manifestation.

2. Recognizing and acknowledging our real personality, the tool that our innerself has given itself for the purpose of creating and manifesting in the physical world.

There may be a time when you feel a need for assistance in the inward journey to face yourself. Select a trained professional to assist you in your growth.

3. Understanding why we play the same patterns over and over again.

4. Moving through all those personality and pattern layers, and then touching the essence, the inner truth and beauty, the all-loving, dimensionless innerself.

The process of Facing Yourself and preparing for an inner dream partner may bring many different facets of one's life into action. Some may be pleasant and some may not. Some may be discarded, others may be kept, and some may need attention.

Before we start on our inward journey, we need to commit to not judging, doubting and/or blaming ourselves, but to simply acknowledging and accepting whatever we discover and whatever we experience as US.

We also have to commit to facing ourselves with integrity, truth, honesty, righteousness, love and compassion. In their totality, those words ask us quite simply to face ourselves without omission of any itsy-bitsy, teeny-weeny part. The outer world teaches us that if a person doesn't ask the right question, we are not obligated to offer a complete answer. This is the very premise of life today; a continual withholding of the "whole honest-to-God truth." It is essential to face ourselves with the "whole honest-to-God truth." Let's not try to fool ourselves, because we really can't. If we face only a part while avoiding or denying awareness of the whole, the innerself knows this devious maneuver and our growth is put into jeopardy. We must face all of ourselves.

To do this may require changing some of the ways we spend our time. We need to create room for our self-discovery, which will probably not take place while we are completely absorbed watching TV, movies, attending parties and so on. It is essential to create time for ourselves and by ourselves. This time can be at home, out in nature, in a church or elsewhere. The important act is to be with ourselves and focus on ourselves.

The first part of our journey in facing ourselves it to look at our mistaken personality which mainly consists of our fears, our self-image and the image we think others have of us. It mistakenly thinks that it is the only important part of the self and that it must survive at all costs. This mistaken personality results from the outer world's domestication, which started with parents and family members and continued with play-mates, friends, teachers, employers and so on. It is the result of our belief systems, of somebody else telling us how to handle our life. We have to grow beyond our mistaken personality in order to have our innerself "run the show" (handle our life).

Have you ever thought about how "inaccurately" we may really communicate with others, and noticed how little of our innerself takes part in that communication?

Follow this example:

1. We see ourselves.

2. We present ourselves.

3. Someone receives our presentation.

4. They interpret their impression of our presentation.

5. They respond with their view of what they interpreted.

6. We receive their presentation.

7. We interpret this information.

8. We decide how accurately we conveyed our message.

These eight human interactions all take place in a matter of seconds!

It is both amazing and ludicrous that so much of what we experience is based on impressions and perceptions.

The next part of our journey in facing ourselves is to acknowledge our real personality, to accept it and to use it as the manifesting tool of our innerself. This manifesting tool is a complex body of traits that could in general be defined as our way of perceiving the world, our method of making things happen, and our way of how we go about deciding our actions, among others. Note that everybody has a different make-up, a different personality and a different way of perceiving things—and again there is no right or wrong, no better or worse. Each and every one of us has exactly the personality needed for our lessons (life experiences) and for our innerselves to manifest in the physical world. *We need to learn to accept our personality and to use it in the appropriate way, namely in cooperation with our innerself.* If we do not, it reverts to the mistaken personality, run by fears and image, which blocks our growth, empowerment and innerself expression.

It is useful to recognize and acknowledge the ego, the part that defines the limits of our personality. It will always be there to some extent because it is through the ego and its use of the senses that we perceive the illusion of separateness, the very essence of making the physical experiences possible. But let's not allow it to run our life!

The next part of our journey involves looking at the patterns we play repeatedly. Let's take a look at our life's experiences, for example, our relationships. We may notice that each experienced relationship appeared different, had a different setting and a different make-up from the others, but the results were the same. Why?—because we operated out of a pattern, a continual, unconscious replay of memories (joyous and painful) stored in our body and activated by our domesticated mind, a pattern that triggers and depends upon our adrenaline flow and its resulting physical and emotional reaction. It is important to release those outer patterns, by forgiving ourselves and the others involved, and to replace them with decisions made in cooperation with our innerself. The innerself needs to be placed firmly in the "driver's seat!"

Do we remember how differently we behaved and reacted as a child? The domestication process was only in its beginning stages and our innerself still worked freely to perceive the world about us and in us. Our childhood expressions most likely came directly from the innerself, a clear, unobstructed presentation of ourselves. *That is what it is all about—getting beyond the domestication, the fears, the patterns, and in touch with the very innerself, the essence. Limiting outer-world influences will enable us to make choices that are in sync with our essence and will assist in manifesting a dream relationship.*

At this point we'll introduce you to two exercises, which you can practice regularly on your own, if they resonate with you and if you feel comfortable doing them. These may help you in discovering and facing yourself.

The first exercise may be used as a beginning tool to establish contact with your innerself, to experience it and to gradually start communicating with it.

The second exercise may be used as a tool for working on yourself in cooperation with your innerself, a tool to help explore and release your patterns, your fears, your image, whatever is obstructing the clear expression of the real you.

EXERCISE 1
Contacting Your Innerself

1. Sit or lie down, relax and breathe gently and deeply with your eyes closed, for three to five minutes.

2. Now ask your innerself to take a form. Accept the first image, feeling or knowing that emerges. You may not actually "see" it, but in some way a form may come to you as a shape, word, sound, smell and/or feeling.

3. Notice the look, feel, smell, and/or sound of the image that comes to you.

4. Gain rapport with your innerself image. Hold it, talk with it, look at it or do whatever seems best to stay with this awareness.

5. Express your unconditional love for the innerself, as represented by the form that has appeared to you.

6. Ask questions and accept what you hear, feel or sense, as YOU, your innerself, communicating.

7. After you've heard your message, be thankful, and then take a few deep breaths and slowly become aware again of your physical presence and surroundings. When you feel ready, slowly open your eyes.

Each time you practice this exercise, you may have a different experience; your innerself may appear in a different shape, sound, smell or other image. Accept whatever you create as being yours. Honor it as being yours, exclusively. With practice, you may gain a comfort level with this exercise. These experiences are a beginning in discovering the beauty, wisdom and unconditional love that dwell in the inner you. Remember, you are a beautiful being!

YOU ARE LOVE—ALL THERE IS.

EXERCISE 2
Discovering and Releasing (patterns, fears, etc.)

1. Sit or lie down, relax and breathe gently and deeply with your eyes closed, for three to five minutes.

2. Ask the innerself to take a form. Accept the first image, feeling or knowing.

3. Gain rapport and perceive this awareness for a few moments.

4. Ask to see, for example, a relationship pattern that is not in sync with your innerself, or a fear, a part of your image, or whatever you choose to work on. Accept what is presented—avoid questioning or attempting to guide a response. Just plain accept the first thing that comes forth.

5. Now look closely at what is presented to you. Accept it, honor it and release it, forgiving yourself and the others involved, and ask your innerself to fill this vacancy with what it feels to be appropriate. This could be love, light, color, sound, shape or other images.

6. After the vacancy is filled, be thankful, and then take a few deep breaths and slowly become aware again of your physical presence and surroundings. When you feel ready, slowly open your eyes.

It is helpful to record what was presented to you in writing as soon as possible after the exercise. Then, over time, you can contemplate these awarenesses for deeper understanding. Often they are "keys" with multiple levels of meaning and application in your life. It is best to proceed slowly rather than to try to discover all the patterns, fears or other limiting factors all at once. Know that they took many years to create. They will take time to release. You will discover a pace that is yours.

EXAMPLE (ALIX). The process of facing myself became easier as my heart opened. It was furthered when I began taking long walks in a nearby forest and was able to relive an important childhood memory—the feeling of nature as a part of me. I was thus reunited with a dear friend. I spent a multitude of weekends alone, without talking to or seeing another person. This gave me an opportunity to face my outer self bit by bit, without judgment, and to acknowledge it with love, compassion and forgiveness. I faced feelings of unworthiness, of being left out, of not being lovable, of my impatience (the fear that there isn't enough time), and of a lack of self-confidence. My mind faced my reasons for entering into relationships, my expectations, my intolerances and on and on. Those were powerful weekends. Each time I felt uplifted, more centered, with greater inner peace. Slowly my domesticated outer self stepped aside and allowed my innerself to get in the "driver's seat" and take charge.

I really wanted to identify and release those deep-seated patterns that interfered with innerself expression. I felt that a deep-rooted releasing would happen best if guided by a professional. In 1989, after reading numerous books about reincarnation, the emotional-body-clearing process and past-life regression, I decided to enter into past-life regression work at a facility in New Mexico. My first eight past-life regression sessions proved to be of great value. I experienced times of touching my painful emotional patterns, and then of allowing myself to release them. I also experienced times of pure ecstasy and bliss, when I touched the essence and felt myself in the oneness of all.

That enormous feeling of freedom, which had permeated my whole being for the first time three and a half years before (after my parents' death), surfaced again. This was the process of freeing myself, of taking away the outer layers and of allowing myself to be the real me. This process would lead to future monumental changes.

EXAMPLE (RONALD). I became aware of how different my innerself was from the outer self as my heart continued to open and was honored, loved and heard. The outer self had become dominant through constant exercise and experience. The innerself was strong, but lacked exercise and experience. All along I had thought that I made my own decisions. No one was going to tell me what to do. During a guided session with a professional, I came to a profound realization: I was not making my decisions; I was rebelling against someone else's decisions. The outer-directed self was playing the game, never letting my innerself say a thing. This reactionary pattern kept me actively participating in an outer game with all my emotions, intellect and physical abilities. I was totally preoccupied. This was a painful acknowledgment and at the same time an inspiring revelation. I observed this behavior and began to use my inner-directed choices, leaving the outer game to those willing to participate.

I had always been comfortable saying yes and giving to others but found it difficult to say no and receive. As a relation-ship began to fail and needed more communication, I usually withdrew into an unspoken state of silence. My normal, com-fortable disposition of giving changed to an uncomfortable indifference and sent the non-verbal message, "I'm not giving; ask me why, and then you decide what to do." The partner generally made the decision to end the relationship and to leave my indifferent behavior. After the break-up, I felt pain and loss from the separation. However, an outer healing began, because the outer reason for my indifference (the failing relationship) was gone. The cowardly act of withdrawal destroyed the relationship, suppressed the expression of my innerself and relinquished my power to the partner. I was afraid to express my innerself. On occasion and through desperation, when my partner did not respond to my withdrawal, I exploded with a burst of frustrated emotion. This acted as a relief valve for my pent-up, denied innerself. Though this outbreak was a sincere and genuinely heart-felt expression, it failed to communicate my message because it was delivered with such frustrated emotion. Later my outer self would discredit the expression of the innerself with various guilt trips. Looking back at this behavior, it became clear to me how divided my smothered innerself was from the outer self.

As I began to express my innerself more frequently, some people I knew became uneasy with this expression. They had accepted my previous, outer-directed behavior but found the expression of my innerself uncomfortable. Some long-time friends faded from my life. This opened opportunities to comfortably express my innerself with new-found friends.

In the continuing process of facing myself, I'm growing from each decision and learning to accept the consequences.

*You may have heard about
the law of like objects being attracted
to one another. This applies here as well.*

Creating Your Dream
Partner

This step could be the last one. However, we choose to introduce it now so that you can continue to work with it as you proceed through the remaining steps. Remember that all the inward steps (five through eleven) are intricately interwoven. When you are working on a current step and uncover some new insight about a preceding step, take the time to understand, absorb and apply it.

Many of us carry or have carried in our mind a fantasy dream partner. Yet we kept it as a fantasy. This process is about discovering our dream partner from the innerself and taking steps to bring that partner into our life. It's time to define the dream partner as the partner who joins us in life's free-flowing dance, who accepts us and gives us permission to be who we inwardly are and who consciously creates with us that "third entity," called the *relationship*, where his/her essence merges with ours, becoming one, and where unconditional love resides.

You may have heard about the law of like objects being attracted to one another. This applies here as well. While finding our way through our mistaken personality and our patterns, we discover more and more who we really are, and we come closer to our essence. *As we become more loving and accepting, the being we really are, attracting our dream partner becomes easier and easier.*

This process of self-discovery and creating and attracting our dream partner must be faced with trust and knowing. We have to trust our innerself, that it will help us attract exactly the partner for whom we are ready. *Our degree of relationship with our innerself, our essence, will determine the degree of dream relationship we can achieve with a partner.* As we have to trust our innerself, we also have to know that we (the innerself) are capable of creating/manifesting that dream partner.

It is essential that we relinquish doubt, because doubt may prohibit us from joining with that dream partner. This process is a lesson in accepting all our successes and all our failures as relevant and valuable. Doubting prohibits us from giving our all. When we don't give our all, the results are diminished, *i.e.,* "If we had done more, it might have worked?" or "We were so close to making it happen; why didn't we try harder?" Let's take a moment to ask ourselves, "What is there to doubt about us?" NOTHING! We need to make our choices, to give our all and just simply do it with ourselves and for ourselves! Creating our dream partner is not a time for doubting.

To create our dream partner, we must be able to conceive of him/her. We suggest that you try the following exercise and experience the fun but, above all, that you keep its importance in mind. This creation is a task of responsibility and a commitment to the innerself. It is a task with the purpose of touching the very innerself and then recognizing choices that are in sync with our essence. This exercise bridges the innerself with the physical outer self.

On a piece of paper write every little detail about your inner dream partner. It can include inner values, likes, favorite activities, a physical description (color of hair, height, weight, etc.), whatever. It is an open concept to be used in a way that you feel best. Writing or typing this description assists in manifesting physically the dream partner—it is a conception, an affirmation.

As you continue going within, as you continue working on the previous and the remaining steps and as you come into contact with your essence, the conception of your dream partner will become clearer. You may have to add and/or delete items from the list over time as your choices become clearer from inside you. This is an ongoing and evolving process.

While you make your list, be careful not to get trapped by outer images and old patterns, by beliefs, desires and expectations. They may hold you exactly where you were before and keep you from the magic of creating and manifesting your dream partner.

When we get to that certain place of unconditional love and acceptance of ourselves, when we recognize and acknowledge the divinity in ourselves and others, when we get in sync with our innerself, trusting it to guide us, a whole new way of perceiving may just open up and the magic will begin.

LET'S LIVE THAT MAGIC!

*It is important for humankind
to get back into the rhythm of the universe—to
agree to and accept change, the very essence
of that rhythm.*

Agreeing to Change

"Will there be change required?" Well, we finally mentioned the proverbial "change" in the title, to save you from suspense.

Agreeing to Change is a key step to a dream relationship. Humans, creatures of habit, sometimes forget that in the whole universe, everything is moving, changing, evolving—nothing is fixed. Think about all that has happened to our home, planet earth since the "beginning of time," how it has transformed, changed and evolved. Species that lived here millions of years ago disappeared and evolved into other forms of existence. Look at nature, the seasons, a never-ending cycle of transformation and change.

Our body, being a part of the whole, is subject to the same changes and transformations. But how many of us accept this changing body? Aren't we trying to do whatever it takes to slow down (even stop) the "aging process," instead of accepting this change and transformation and learning from it. It is just another lesson on our journey.

Everything is energy and energy is fluid, not to be captured and fixed at one specific moment in time. Humans, trapped in the illusion called time, developed the calendar at one specific moment in "time," taking into account the knowledge at that particular moment. The calendar is a very rigid structure and appears more and more to be out of sync with the fluidity of the universe. This rigid structure nevertheless remains the reference for the change of seasons and so on. If, for example the first snow falls in October and the first spring flowers bloom in February, we think the weather is acting crazy. It may never cross our mind that the calendar might simply not be in harmony with the rhythm of the universe. We don't deny that a multitude of stimuli influence our weather patterns. However, let's give some thought to those human-created, rigid structures that don't allow room for change, transformation and evolution.

A few years ago we bought a "Christmas-cactus," so called because it blooms for Christmas. Over the years our "Christmas-cactus" has changed; it blooms for Thanksgiving, Christmas, Valentine's Day, Easter, Memorial Day and who knows when. Humans try to categorize things to fit into one particular period. Nature, however, in its universal flow, responds to energies that we cannot control, of which we are unaware and which don't fit into a rigid structure.

It is important for humans to get back into the rhythm of the universe—to agree to and accept change, the very essence of that rhythm.

Yes, change is a very simple word to say but generally a very difficult word to define and implement, until we develop a system that works for us. How many times have we been unhappy with a relationship, our job, whatever? Inside us was a knowing that something wasn't working and that it needed to be changed. Our mind found hundreds of excuses not to change, such as, "The family thinks the world of my partner"; "I know my current partner; I may not get another"; "This is a great-paying job"; "People respect me for what I do." Our mind makes the decision to remain and "hopes" that somebody may eventually change and cause us to feel better. That other somebody will not bring us the appropriate change, peace or happiness. The only person with that potential is each and every one of us. It is our own responsibility and not to be delegated to others.

Many of us resist change internally and find it difficult to let go of our resistance. However, guess what?—if we have no resistance, we experience no harm. Have you tried to hit your fist against a stone wall? Have you tried to hit your fist against the wind? The results of these actions clearly show us the potential harm in resistance. It may be helpful to think about this example when we are confronted with and/or have the opportunity to initate change, as we do have in the eleven-step process.

An underlying cause that makes us resist change and at the same time controls us, is FEAR. Fear is a main outer obstacle to change, transformation, development, growth, empowerment and on and on . . . as well as to freedom. The moment we remove this main outer obstacle and replace fear-motivated behavior with love-motivated behavior, we open up to our inner, limitless potential. What is fear? It is that feeling of anxiety, apprehension and concern that makes life's choices difficult to cope with. Fear makes up part of our mistaken personality as seen in Step Seven. It might be masked as impatience (the fear of not having enough time), greed (the fear of not having enough), self-deprecation (the fear of not being good enough), or other negative emotions. Fear is a hurdle we have to jump over in order to manifest our whole potential, to become free. *By going further and further within, we get in touch with our innerself, and by agreeing to change and to again becoming a conscious part of that universal flow, we overcome our resistance, our fear, and we become free to manifest our potential. We will have no reason to fear as we get to know and trust our innerself and to recognize the divine in us, letting it guide us.*

Another resistance to change is attachment, which in itself is another fear (the fear of loss). Human beings are attached to material things, people, situations, memories, their lives and their patterns, and they struggle to keep everything exactly the way they have it or remember it, fixed in a moment of time. The continual movement of the universe requires that everything in it move as well. If we try to resist, to keep everything at a fixed moment, we are like a rubber band caught on a post, and we become stretched out of our natural, relaxed shape. The nature of a rubber band is to try to maintain its relaxed shape. Change is inevitable and our resistance grabs us at various points, stretching us (forcing discomfort) as our essence labors to retain its shape. What happens when the rubber band breaks or gets suddenly released? We get catapulted into the change that we have been resisting and we might experience an extremely hard awakening. Within the universal flow, it is inevitable that change will occur at some point, and we may feel terribly hurt when we experience the change or the so-called "loss." We may not realize that our own attachment, our resistance to change, brought about the hurt. The very thing we were most afraid of or had the most resistance to—loss, or change, happened.

It is crucial to discover what we need to change and not to wait for outer circumstances to decide our change for us. We may do this by accepting our sincere choices, as guided by the innerself, and then by taking the appropriate actions to effect those changes. At first it may take time to weed through the symptoms to get to an understanding of what needs to be changed. Remember, we are creating an outer self from the innerself. This is a self-reliant method that we can adjust according to our inner knowing. To attune to the innerself's guidance as to what changes are needed or appropriate, continue practicing the exercises described in Step Seven, Facing Yourself. With each change we need to be prepared to accept whatever will be required to accomplish our chosen results. We need to allow the changes to happen. Changes will occur automatically, without attention, or from a concentrated effort. Some will be subtle, some natural, and some dramatic as we follow the eleven-step process. Often the effort and time to change may seem endless, however we must "break rocks" to build and achieve our just rewards.

Way too often, the decision to change is forced by or solely based on outer choices. This fuels a treadmill life and causes an ever-widening separation from the innerself. The agreed-to outer changes are most often conditional and in turn bring on fears of not meeting those conditions.

As we go through various stages of outer changes in this lifetime, there are times when we think we have deservedly earned the right for the next change to be easier—that there has been an earned right to jump from the top of our current achievement to the top of our next chosen endeavor. Well, not quite.

Let's take a look at how some segments of the outer world direct our change. Some outer-world choices have borders, and within those borders are defined methods of making change. For the following example the arena of change will be a job choice, represented by a ladder. This change begins by an actual search for the appropriate opportunity and results in finding a group (company) that accepts us, and we accept it. Next, we learn the job's responsibilities and how to successfully perform at a level that ensures an acceptable rate of advancement into additional responsibilities and/or rewards. With our success comes attention from those who benefit from these achievements, and the need to invoke political considerations. Those who supervise ask for their needs to be met. Those supervised ask for their needs to be met. We have the tendency to heedlessly listen to our supervisors because they can pull us up the ladder, while the intent of the innerself gets completely neglected. Our supervisors like continued success and encourage us to follow them more closely, causing increasing dependency and obedience. Through this conscientious and attentive behavior, we arrive at the top, just in time to replace the retiring supervisor. At the top, the distance between us and those being supervised is vast and the intent of the innerself remains unheard. Suddenly fear strikes us. It is an awareness of not knowing how we reached this point. We are unable to recognize our support, and we miss the reliance on the retired supervisor. Now, others follow and listen to our every word, waiting for us to retire.

The above illustrates the fast track to the top. However, if we decide not to take the fast track and pause anywhere along the way, we may notice our fears immediately. We may feel these fears in a variety of ways as early as at the entry level position, *e.g.,* "Will I get laid off?" Fear is the key ingredient, a common thread, in keeping this outer-world ladder working. Fear promotes making immediate decisions without any innerself input and can be called a "fear jerk" reaction to the immediacy of the outer situation.

Meanwhile, back at the top, we have little room to move. And what do we feel like?—a sitting duck! To the left, right and all around, is down. Fear kicks in with the "fear jerk" reaction, "Leave and choose another ladder." The next ladder gives the signal to "come on over" and we begin our jump with the intent to reach the top spot, because it's the place we feel we've earned, based on the performance on the current ladder. In mid-air, we discover that the new ladder has another set of rules and that our intended leap is going to fall short of that top rung.

This is the type of outer change we often experience. On this march to the top we did not take one second to have that all-important conference with our innerself. We were completely absorbed by and agreeable to the required outer-directed messages. Many segments of the outer world require that we meet specific prerequisites in order for our changes to occur.

We ascribe here to getting in touch with our innerself's universally-guided recommendations for change. Inner-motivated change comes from a place of inner trust, not fear. While making changes it is essential to always maintain complete inner integrity. By building a firm base of sincere intent and loving attention, we may avoid the traps of the outer world's rigid structures that continually prod and lure us. We need to love and appreciate this inner process and to accept equally our successes and failures.

Our eleven-step process is about changing the outer-directed perception of ourselves to become the very innerself. We need to trust our innerself because it knows best and is in sync with the universal flow. The outer self manifests this trust through our experiences in the physical world. Let's trust our heart, the altar of the innerself.

EXAMPLE (ALIX). I was born and had always lived in Luxembourg, Europe. In August 1989, I arrived in New Mexico to do my first past-life regression sessions and drove a rented car to my destination. When I stepped out of the car I started crying and a little voice inside me said, "You are home!!!" I truly felt a sense of being home during those three weeks in New Mexico. My interpretation of the words of that little voice at that time was appropriate, because it was a part of the path that led me to where I had to be. Only much later did I come to the profound realization that the true meaning of these three little words, "You are home," was far beyond my interpretation of that time: *I had come home within myself !* After the past-life regression sessions, I was so aware of the feeling of being free. My process approached a culmination where something major was going to change in my life.

Before leaving, I decided that upon my return to Luxembourg, I would sell my possessions and then come back to New Mexico. My mind didn't know how my life would work out, but my heart knew New Mexico was home. Something greater than the outer-directed me was at work. I did not have mind chatter or doubt about this decision; I had only trust. On September 1, 1989, I arrived in Luxembourg, left my job, sold my belongings and let my friends and remaining family know of my decision. Some people didn't say a word; some told me I was crazy to leave such a respected, well-paying job and to give up all the beautiful material comforts; some suggested professional counseling; some admitted they would love to do the same thing (change their whole life) but didn't have the courage to do so; some were very puzzled by the new attraction they felt towards me and noticed my inner peace, freedom and knowing; and some were curious and questioned me on how I was making this transition. My best friend of more than twenty years was very happy for me and gave me all the loving support and help I needed. She did this without a complete understanding and later confided that she was actually very concerned about my decision to make this all-encompassing, worldly change. Everything went smoothly.

On November 30, 1989, I left Luxembourg with two suitcases for the United States of America. My innerself was manifesting in the outer world. The trust in my inner knowing continued the real manifestation. In February 1990, I met Ronald (see my example in Step Ten). We went out for the first time on March 15, had a seven-hour talk about our lives in April and were amazed at the incredible similarities. The 2nd of June

Ronald proposed to me and we were married on the 22nd of September 1990. It was all so simple. The unconditional trust in my innerself had brought about a reward beyond my most audacious dreams—a dream relationship realized in unconditional love.

EXAMPLE (RONALD). I had learned to focus on my goals and to achieve them at all costs. My move to San Francisco was a move from the heart. I loved San Francisco and decided that it would be my last stop. Many people commented that I was probably one of the best ambassadors to the City. San Francisco was a heart-felt utopia. Needless to say, it fit me. In September, 1989 I visited New Mexico to do past-life regression sessions. Does this sound familiar? These sessions reopened my heart and allowed me to see from the inside out. Everything was very appealing about New Mexico and my heart told me to stay. When I returned to San Francisco, my heart didn't change its feelings about New Mexico and kept telling me to move. My mind tried to kick in and offer reasons to stay in San Francisco—friends, home, beautiful area, connections and so on. My heart picked up the phone and I scheduled a return visit to New Mexico for two weeks in December 1989 to see if this was really a true, heart-felt message. After those two weeks and on the return plane ride to San Francisco, my mind got the message to start doing what had to be done to make the move. I began by telling my friends and received some of the same reactions that Alix experienced. People couldn't believe I was leaving and thought there would come a time when I would change my mind and stay.

In February 1990 I visited New Mexico again to rent an apartment where I met Alix. I returned to San Francisco, sold most of my belongings, and bid my farewells. Inside me, it was my time to move and the obstacles that surfaced were quickly disposed of without a struggle. I arrived in New Mexico in

March 1990, was engaged to Alix in June and we were married in September. It happened that easily because I had listened to my innerself and had agreed to change.

We need to gently remove any self-limiting thoughts and replace them with our fondest innermost dreams.

Opening Your Borders

It is time to open our borders! The outer world enslaves us to be goal-directed and teaches that goals are reached with tunnel vision. It may be likened to wearing blinders, which prohibit us from seeing those important little signs along our life's path that indicate the appropriate way to our satisfaction, prosperity, happiness, love and friendship.

Many times our mind develops a detailed plan to achieve a goal. The mind insists we adhere to the plan without concessions and establishes the borders. The mind has been educated and conditioned through outer experiences, accepts them and uses us to validate them. This appears to be a very limited approach, for it often neglects the innerself and the infinite number of other physical and metaphysical possibilities.

Today many of our knowings focus on what we can't do, because we have been told over and over again that certain things are impossible. Our mind accepts those limitations and creates the borders that prohibit us from magic and miracles.

Yet, *they are possible!* Many of us have been correctly told since we were children that fire burns and hurts and that we should keep away from it. That's what our mind accepts and that is our created "border," or our fear about fire. We can tell you now (see Alix's example) that with the appropriate preparation and instructions we *can* walk on fire, on glowing coals, without burning or hurting our feet. *The moment we open our border (overcome our fear) by "reprogramming" our mind that it is possible, IT WILL BE. We reach that place beyond our mind, where magic and miracles are possible—the infinite, dimensionless innerself.*

When we release those mind prejudices and predetermined judgments, and when we listen to our heart, then act through our mind, we will have fun discovering the ways that the universal laws of unlimited opportunity and choice work with us. We will notice that it is a cooperative journey, not a fight.

Our goals are important and we need to move towards them. Too often we drive towards the goal at all costs. Know that many chosen goals come into our lives so that we can learn a lesson. The lesson may come early in the goal-driven course, so that to attain the goal may serve no real purpose. Let's move toward our goals, yet still allow other opportunities to present themselves. When the time is right, new opportunities surface and present new goals that resonate with our innerself. Then we need to agree to change and leave the current goal to pursue the new one.

Due to our impatience, we often miss the all-important universal timing (we're either too early or too late), *e.g.*, "I can't wait"; "Hurry up"; "There isn't enough time"; "I'll do just one more thing," and all those types of anxiety-driven modes.

Also, we need to allow an opportunity for the universal timing of all events that are necessary for our growth and well-being to enter our life experiences. Many of us have experienced how some choices we made reached fruition so easily, and how some choices became a continual hassle and struggle. Well, the easy ones were in sync with our innerself, with the universal timing of events meant for our experience, and we outwardly acted them out. The difficult ones were strictly an outer choice established by others that we agreed to do. It may have worked for them. We may have helped it work for them. They may have convinced our outer self it was best for us. However, deep inside (deep because we have ignored it for so long), we sensed something wasn't quite right. Instead of following that inner knowing, we were outwardly driven toward achieving the goal. There is a balance to choosing, continuing and releasing goals. When we are so preoccupied with achieving a difficult goal, the universal timing of our inner-agreeable events cannot reach us. We haven't allowed appropriate time for them to occur. Instead, we have jam-packed our life so tightly that nothing can enter that isn't in our treadmill routine. We are running here, there and everywhere and going nowhere fast.

If we can reach a balance of inner choices, then act them out in the outer world, we can bring about a whole and satisfying life experience. Balance is so very important in order to acquire and maintain a healthy, happy, peaceful and loving life. Balance is our place of power. While at this center—balance—we can clearly and comfortably recognize our choices and reach appropriate decisions. Here our various attributes are joined in a pleasing harmony. Our borders are open to welcome—and prepared to accept—whatever life has to offer.

The Importance of Balance

What do we mean by balance?

Our personal Teeter Totter Analogy illustrates the importance we've recognized in remaining centered and within ourselves.

The characters in our Teeter Totter Analogy include: Charly, who represents the human being in all its splendor.

We present to you—Charly.

The Platform,
which represents the continually-moving life path
on which experiences are met.

The Triangle,
the pinnacle of which identifies the most centered and
balanced place to be for meeting life's experiences.

The following captioned illustrations represent Charly's experiences while learning the importance of balance.

1. Charly begins at center point, which provides for a level path. This is a position of strength, as well as the point where Charly can most effectively handle all that life has to offer. Charly's key is to remain here and accept life's challenges and rewards from this place of self-empowerment.

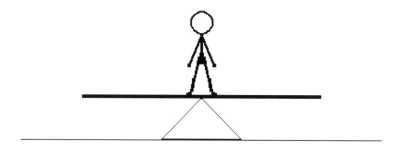

2. Okay, Charly, you're aware of a joyful experience approaching. Unfortunately, Charly's impatience to experience this joy takes over, causing Charly to lose sight of that self-empowering center. Note how, by moving towards this joyful experience, Charly ends up lower than center. Also, each step to hurry towards this experience is a step away from Charly's place of strength. Charly will indeed experience the joy earlier, but at an expensive price! Charly used a lot of energy to gain the experience while away from center, and will require even more energy returning to center. If Charly had remained at center, far less energy would have been used and it would have provided an excellent position from which to meet life's next experience.

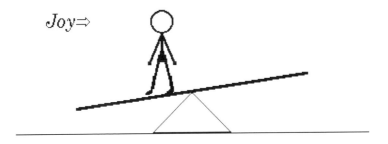

3. This time, aware of a great joy approaching, Charly's impatience explodes. With complete abandonment of center, Charly flies up and forward, hurrying to meet it. Charly uses an immense amount of personal resources to get there fast.

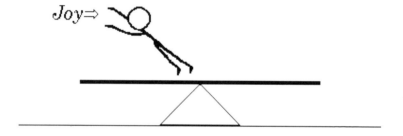

4. The elation from the joyful experience ends, as do all good things, returning Charly, literally "down-and-out," to the life path. Going down happens much faster than going up. Gravity has a way of harshly teaching the off-centered.

5. Super Star Charly has gone very high, very far and fallen very fast. Our star will have a most difficult journey back to center. (This happens many times with public figures.) Charly recklessly attempted to be at the top of an arena, abandoning center, only to come crashing down. Dazed and out-of-sorts, Charly keeps looking up to where the fall started. Charly asks, "Why me?" only to hear the outer world echo back, "Why meee? Why meee? Why meee? . . ." Charly left and forgot that place of center and strength where all answers dwell.

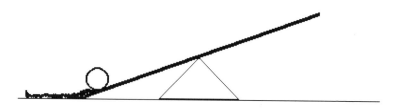

6. Charly's venture far and away from center requires a whole lot of time and effort in order to return there. Remember, this is what can happen by rushing a joyful experience. Many of us have overindulged in a joyful experience, only to feel down and empty afterwards. Charly needs to practice remaining at center, "enjoying," and then letting go.

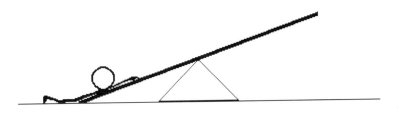

7. Okay, Charly, on the horizon is a difficult experience approaching, sorrow.

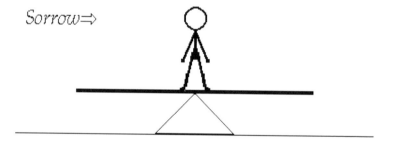

8. Charly recognizes the approaching sorrow and decides to postpone it by backing away from it. With each avoiding step backward, Charly inches lower and further from center.

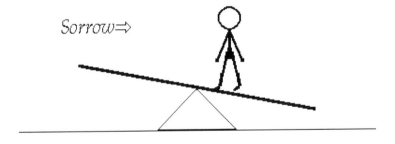

Sorrow⇒

9. Now, even further and lower from center, Charly is stressed and falsely convinced of avoiding this sorrow. Charly *hopes* the sorrow will pass right on by.

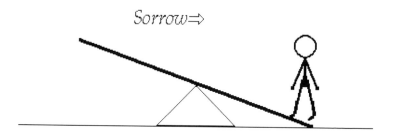

10. Charly decides to take up hiding. Sorry, Charly, there is no avoiding your life experiences. This sorrowful experience will seek you out wherever you may be hiding. In fact, Charly is now well below the experience, stressed and anxious, hoping for it to pass. But sorrow follows gravity's call, falling hard and fast to join Charly.

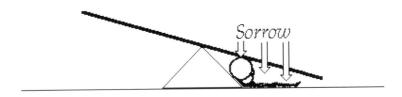

11. Stressed and exhausted from the experience of avoidance, Charly wrestles through the sorrow from a place of weakness. But hark! On the horizon another joyful experience approaches. Unfortunately, from this low point, Charly is completely unable to see it (there'll be no rushing to meet "joy" this time). The joy looks for Charly at the expected, universally-agreed-upon center, only to discover Charly missing. The joy moves past center, notices Charly, and they join at a point low and away from center. Meeting at a point lower than center has a neutralizing effect on the joyous experience. For example, Charly is energized by, inspired by and loves to hear musician "A." The joyful experience (an opportunity to attend an "A" concert) approaches Charly while at this low point. Charly attends the "A" concert and is only slightly elevated. Charly is disappointed that "A didn't quite have it that night." While at a low point, even the best of life's experiences can be disappointing.

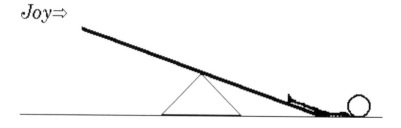

12. Charly has a truly difficult time regaining center. It is an uphill climb (as it was from over-excitement) that requires a lot of effort and energy. Charly is beginning to learn that maintaining center is much less strenuous and much more rewarding than plunging off either end when meeting life's experiences.

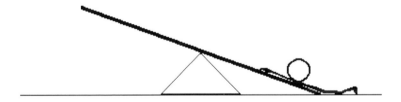

13. Congratulations, Charly! You've learned the value of remaining centered as well as the immense difficulties that result from rushing or postponing. Charly is now meeting life's rewarding and challenging experiences from the appropriate time and place, center.

**Thank you, Charly, for showing us
that instruction is a reminder,
experience is a teacher and
action is a necessity.**

As Charly demonstrated, ***Opening Your Borders is critically consequential because it places us in sync and in balance with the infinite universal flow of potentially beneficial events.***

While we experiment with finding our balance in life, it is helpful to realize that the outer self often creates another border called a mask. We may find someone else appealing and attempt to copy him/her, only we end up with a mask. The mask becomes a block for the expression of the specific needs of our innerself. Each of us is unique! By becoming self-confident and discovering what dwells inside, we can escape the outer mask and no longer act out a disguised role uncomfortably from behind the mask.

This is a good time to be reminded that all our thoughts are like prayers. For example, when we frequently think, "I am not worthy," that thought will manifest. It attracts to us people and situations to prove that thought. The thought, "I am worthy," will attract to us people and situations to prove that thought. The choice is ours to create our own reality. We need to gently remove any self-limiting thoughts and replace them with our fondest innermost dreams. Open Your Borders!

EXAMPLE (ALIX). I cherish this experience deeply. It demonstrates how my mind and heart worked. Ronald and I met early in February 1990 at the rental office of an apartment complex where I was living. I was there to pay my rent and Ronald came in to rent a place. The manager introduced us and asked me to show Ronald my place, since he was interested in a unit that was going to be available that had the same floor plan as mine. We talked a little about what had brought us to New Mexico and discovered that our reasons were the same. Ronald said that after he got settled in March, he would call to get together for dinner. A few days later, we met again at a meditation group. Ronald said he had taken an apartment at another complex and would arrive there in early March.

Late on the afternoon of March 15, Ronald called to ask if I would like to go to the library with him that evening to experience a woman channel. Now, pay special attention to what happened to me in the next few seconds before answering Ronald. My mind's chatter said, "What am I going to do there? Will it be boring? It is already late afternoon. How am I going to manage all the things I have to do and be ready on time? It might be better to tell him to get together another time." While my mind did all this chatter, that little voice inside kept saying, "Just Go!!!" Then I heard myself say to Ronald, "Okay, what time will you be by to pick me up?" I was able to experience the prelude of our dream relationship because my heart had opened my borders.

My first fire walk was another wonderful example of opening my borders. Like most people I had been correctly taught that fire burns and hurts, but as the opportunity of a fire walk was given to me, I was willing to give it a try. It happened on Good Friday of 1990—I couldn't think of a more meaningful day. The whole preparation (several hours) before the actual walk was a very special and sacred time. Then I did it—I even walked twice—and my feet were perfect; nothing had apparently changed on the physical level, but doors had flung open on other levels. I can hardly find words to describe the experience. I had gone beyond the "borders" and reached that place of magic where anything is possible. The best way to describe it would probably be: I felt the whole universe in me, a very, very powerful experience that changed me noticeably, even on a physical level, as I heard the next day. The next morning I called Ronald to wish him well for a meeting he had that day (see Ronald's example). He told me his meeting had been canceled and invited me to spend the day with him. Then he said, "By the way, your voice sounds so different—what happened?" I told him about my fire walk. His first reaction was, "I want to see your feet."

EXAMPLE (RONALD). So many times I refused to take no for an answer. I spent a great amount of time and energy attempting to make something work, only to find out that if it did happen, it was a horrible experience. When it didn't work, I got angry, upset and lived in this state for some time. This kept me from seeing and participating in experiences beneficial to my growth.

I can think of no better or more important example of me opening my borders than what follows. Upon moving to New Mexico, I learned of a prominent and world-recognized woman in the field of metaphysics who lived there. I called her and she agreed to meet with me after two weeks' time. I was looking forward to that day. Well, the day of the appointment, just minutes before I was to leave, she called to cancel (due to illness). She nevertheless offered to meet with me if it was absolutely necessary. My heart expressed concern for her speedy recovery, that she take good care of herself and that we would meet at a time she felt appropriate. I hung up the phone, disappointed, but what was more important, concerned for her. I had thoughts like, "It was so great of her to offer to get together despite her poor health; I hope she has a good health care specialist." My phone rang; it was Alix. We had been out for dinner, about a week before, and she was calling to wish me a good meeting today. I explained that it had been canceled and that I would probably do a little exploring around New Mexico. I invited her to join me. We spent the day together and it proved to be the beginning of our dream relationship. This is an example of how I didn't get upset with my disappointing news, but instead was in a place to ask Alix to join me for the day. I was opening my borders.

STEP 11

*In order for us to be
the innerself, that free-flowing, unobstructed
river, the outer self needs to step aside and
allow time for our journey within.*

Going With YOUR Flow

We emphasize *YOUR* flow to bring the attention to the process of your inner-directed awareness. Wouldn't it be wonderful to discard things that we continue to do and yet can't remember why, or which we do not feel comfortable doing? It is our choice—a choice to look inside and then make a decision. We may in fact experience a potential we never dreamed existed, an inner wisdom.

Let's think of our innerself as being like a wave on a body of crystal clear water, let's say a river, representing the oneness. What is a wave? The water rises up and it is water; the water falls back and it is still water. So, what is the difference between the wave and the water? NONE. There is no separation from the water, even though somebody made up the "separating" name, "wave."

Our flow, our innerself (the wave), is part of the universal flow (the river) and at the same time *is* the universal flow. This may make it clear to us why we touch our limitless potential—that place of creation and magic, our universal knowing and wisdom—as soon as we get within our flow and go with it.

Let's continue with the analogy of being a wave or, better yet, as we just demonstrated, the water in the river of oneness. What happens to some of the water of this river on its journey? It gets caught in eddies. And what is the consequence of being caught in an eddy? The water goes in circles, around and around and around, and it may take an extraordinary occurrence for the water to get back "on course," to get back to its unobstructed flow.

Each of us probably can identify what those eddies are in our river. Yes, they are our belief systems, our imprinting, our image, our fears, our borders, our judgments and prejudices, our resistance to change and our domesticated mind, which is reluctant to work with the flow of our river, due to its outer-world marching orders. When our mind is presented with change, it firmly defines the borders, how the change will take place and its outcome. This limits the possibilities and keeps us right in our eddies.

The segments of the outer-directed world that are not in sync with our innerself ask us to join with them, play by their rules, and attract us to the eddies. This begins in our childhood. Parents give their children what is comfortable for the parents. As the child grows and begins to share its gift of the innerself, at times the child is directed by the parents' choice. When we start school, teachers and schoolmates continue to direct us toward outer choices, sometimes trapping us in an eddy. As an adult, our employer determines a means of behavior for us to exist in the outer world. During all these years of experience, each influence attempts to bring us to a particular consensus of outer-directed behavior. Everyone proclaims to know what is best for us, luring us away from the unobstructed flow of our river. We lack the instruction and encouragement needed to stay in this unobstructed flow. It is this outer-directed learning, designed by others, that determines our behavior and ideas of success and failure and sometimes deposits us in another eddy.

How do we get out of our eddies and back into the unobstructed flow of our river? It might be very difficult, because the outer world and its domestication is so predominant. The outer world has required conformity while suppressing opportunities to provide assistance in looking inward and in being able to self-discover a comfort level and contributory role in the world. *In order to get back into the unobstructed flow of our river, we need to agree to initiate change from the inside and to let the answers unfold without premeditated expectations.* We suggest a self-determined, motivated behavior in returning to our unobstructed flow, rather than being forced by a dramatic, outer-directed occurrence, *e.g.*, having to change a destructive habit, or learning of a life-threatening illness, divorce, or death of a loved one.

Our experiences taught us to let go of our borders, limitations, judgments and prejudices and to go beyond our fears and outer images. We have learned to be centered, to take life as it comes, to decide our choices from inside and to make them happen with our outer skills. We gained trust in our innerself and surrender to its guidance.

THIS IS OUR WAKE-UP CALL!

In order for us to be the innerself, that free-flowing, unobstructed river, the outer self needs to step aside and allow time for our journey within. There are generally no blueprints for this journey. Each of us is designing our own. When we get out of our eddies and back into our flow, we discover our purpose, our potentials and being one with the river of oneness. *When the innerself flows, and when the outer self acts to manifest, we are alive and living all we can be.*

EXAMPLE (ALIX ∞ RONALD). In Step Nine we agreed to change and allowed change to happen. In Step Ten we opened our borders. In Step Eleven we met the challenge to get out of our eddies and back into the unobstructed flow of our river. Our innerselves asked us to leave Luxembourg and California and go to New Mexico. The innerself directed these choices (flow). We were able to release the segments of the outer world that controlled our experiences. Doubts were absent. Our mind was in sync with the innerself and led us to take the appropriate actions. We trusted and surrendered to something greater, our innerselves, the universal flow.

After we came together, we recognized that our innerselves had guided us to meet, and that was the reason for us coming to New Mexico. All the other reasons that we had accepted along the way as being the reasons had been a necessary part of the path to bring us together. We had abandoned our eddies and were in our flow. Our joining unfolded at the appropriate time and we continue to walk our life's path,

"Always Together!"

Closing Message

Now, that you have read through the eleven steps, you have come to understand that a way to get to the pinnacle of the triangle—YOUR DREAM RELATIONSHIP—is through a very close relationship with the innerself.

While going through this eleven-step process, we may have times when the decisions of the innerself are in disagreement with the worldly presence of the outer self. It is important not to be swayed at these points on our journey, such as when people we currently know meet our changes with a variety of reactions. Some may try their best to keep us as we are. Some may reject us and walk away, slowly or immediately. Some may become fascinated with the "new us." Some may express the desire to learn from us, while others closely observe our new behavior. We need to accept all with love and without judgment, whatever their reactions might be, and to respect them for whatever degree of awareness they have. A key is to keep focused on our own process and to be grateful and inspiring to others through our loving and accepting ways.

Remember that judgment (of ourselves and others) is not a part of this process. It causes the very opposite of what we are striving for. It causes separation, while the very core of a dream relationship is oneness. We have written throughout the eleven steps about the domestication of the mind, the outer image, the outer world's messages, and the imprinting by parents, friends, teachers, and so on. This isn't intended to contain any judgment, but is simply an acknowledgment to promote the awareness of the existence of those valuable lessons that are presented to us by the outer world. The outer world is the reality we all have created. Our innerself has been inside all the time and awaits us to come "home." Let's take that opportunity and go "home" to become at one with ourselves.

We have to know and also accept that the pieces of our life's puzzle are those belonging to many different people. We are in turn a piece in their puzzle. As we become increasingly aware of who we are, as we make more and more changes to get in sync with our innerself, changes that are without the consent of others, the design of our puzzle will naturally change. Some existing pieces will no longer fit, as for example people who look at life and at our process in a negative way, who don't support us during our development, or who only try to discourage us. New pieces, for example people on the same "wave length" who will support us on our path, and, when we're prepared and ready, A DREAM PARTNER, will be attracted to fill the vacancies in our puzzle. We need to remember that it is important to let go of the "old" in order to attract and make room for the "new." The piece we have occupied in somebody else's puzzle may no longer fit and thus cause us to leave.

YES, this process is challenging; it is not a cake walk and it asks for full effort and commitment.

Before you begin to experience and live the eleven-step process, we want to emphasize that *it is most important to let go of the outcome.* Remember the "rainbow-colored bubble" we used in the introduction. We sincerely mean it: you need to place *YOUR* dream relationship in that beautiful, rainbow-colored, imaginary bubble and release it to fly free, to merge with the universal flow, knowing that it will come back when you are ready. The key is to enjoy the process, the journey, and always know that, even if there are many challenges to be met, and even if it is a course of change that will employ all of your determination and effort, the rewards may well be beyond any possible imagination.

On this journey within, you may have a multitude of bright new experiences that encourage you to continue on. It is a journey "home"—to your innerself. As you come to experience that realization, you'll know that you can create YOUR DREAM RELATIONSHIP and that this journey "home" will have made a difference in your life, a difference in other people's lives, and a difference in the world.

May the vows of our dream relationship be of inspiration to you:

We, Alix ∞ Ronald, recognize:

♥ *our infinite divine connections.*

♥ *our innerselves as pure channels.*

♥ *our essences as being here to overcome the limitations of our outer selves and the outer world.*

We, Alix ∞ Ronald:

♥ *give each other permission to be who we inwardly are and to allow the free-flowing dance of our beings.*

♥ *love our bodies unconditionally and use them to manifest our innerselves in the outer world.*

♥ *draw our attention from our outer selves to our innerselves where peace, joy and wonder dwell.*

♥ *strive to make our way back from the illusion of separateness to the oneness.*

♥ *open our borders and merge into the universal flow.*

♥ *search for indication, not explanation, without being dependent upon words and letters.*

We, Alix ∞ Ronald, choose to:

♥   *acknowledge the oneness that unites us all.*

♥   *live in harmony with the Earth and all Creations.*

♥   *expand and elevate our frequencies.*

♥   *always live in unconditional love.*

♥   *give all to all.*

♥   *help people understand that they can decide their changes.*

♥   *perform synchronous development work.*

♥   *bring spiritual practice into our daily lives.*

♥   *live in the moment.*

♥   *be always aware of the infinite possibilities.*

♥   *silence our minds and listen to our innerselves.*

♥   *keep our spiritual joining in front of our life choices.*

We, Alix ∞ Ronald, choose a life forever together, and ask God that, through openness and surrender, our minds work in synchronicity with our joining spirits.